FAITH
AND LAW

FAITH
AND LAW

Juridical
Perspectives
for the
Ecumenical
Movement

Marc Reuver

WCC Publications, Geneva

To Konrad Raiser,
who encouraged me
to do this study

Cover design: Rob Lucas

ISBN 2-8254-1325-9

© 2000 WCC Publications, World Council of Churches
150 route de Ferney, Box 2100
1211 Geneva 2, Switzerland

Web site: http://www.wcc-coe.org

Printed in Switzerland

You shall love the Lord your God with all your heart,
with all your soul, and with all your might.
And these words which I command you today shall be in your heart;
you shall teach them diligently to your children,
and shall talk of them when you sit in your house,
when you walk by the way, when you lie down, and when you rise up.
(Deut. 6:5-7)

Table of Contents

Foreword

In 1974, the Faith and Order commission received and discussed a recommendation on the issue of the ecumenical movement and church law. While ecumenical discussions had concentrated on issues of doctrine and worship as the most obvious causes for the division of the church, and the most potent factors in sustaining that division, it was seen as important that discussion now focus also on constitutional and legal issues.

The recommendation noted a series of factors which made a discussion of the topic timely. Among the several factors which pointed in the direction of the necessity of treating this topic were the need to modify rules and regulations in the churches to reflect the ecumenical agreements reached through theological dialogues. Condemnations crafted in a different period were seen in some cases no longer to be applicable, and yet they remained enshrined in church law. New representative systems which had been called forth by the ecumenical instruments had not been envisaged in the framing of practices and procedures adopted in a different situation. The agreements reached in ecumenical discussions needed to be embedded in the constitutions of the churches, particularly where these involved the incorporation of new confessions of faith or changes in the discipline in the churches. The issue was also an important one for those churches which sought to enter church union schemes, where a variety of church polities needed to be rationalized, and where church law was frequently invoked by minorities who did not wish to move towards church union.

While the recommendation for work in this area was adopted by the commission, it proved impossible to proceed further with it, due to limited resources of staff and finance. After the passage of a quarter of a century where this topic has not been pursued, it is even more urgent that a discussion on it be opened. There are a plethora of agreements reached by churches through multilateral and bilateral dialogues in different regional, national and local contexts which need to be incorporated into the constitutions of the different churches. These very dialogues have helped the churches to move into new relationships. The churches require new ways of expressing those relationships and embodying them in their life, if they are to allow the relationship to progress. Without this, the agreements reached will be marginalized and the very process of ecumenical dialogue called into question.

Further, because of the developing relations between churches and their commitment to the search to manifest as fully as possible their growing real but imperfect communion, no church can assume that it can legislate as an internal matter without it having its impact on the perceptions and developing relations with its ecumenical partners.

This volume is an attempt to open up a conversation on this topic. In broad brush strokes, the historical development of the nature and parameters of church law and canon law are presented. The relation between the theology of the different confessional traditions and their polity is outlined and discussed. This has been approached, as the recommendation for the plenary commission at Accra suggested, in a comparative manner. This approach has the value of allowing the different ways of configuring the relationship to emerge, and to give some account of the ethos of the different confessions.

Obviously, within the scope of the volume it has not been possible to be exhaustive in examining every possible church tradition in depth. The author has, however, drawn on the current substantial literature available on the different churches and has managed to present a study which allows a further substantive discussion to take place within and between the different churches. He has further opened up the important discussion on addressing social, economic, political and moral questions – issues which in some polities pertain to the discipline of the church. This volume therefore is a timely and important contribution to ecumenical discussion, and it is to be hoped that the issues it raises will be the subject of common reflection and action.

ALAN D. FALCONER
Director
Faith and Order Commission
World Council of Churches

Introduction

In 1974 the Faith and Order Commission of the World Council of Churches published an Outline concerning *The Ecumenical Movement and Church Law*. Its focus was the need for the updating of church law to match the new realities of the ecumenical movement. While ecumenical discussion had largely centred on doctrine and worship as the areas in which the division of the church was most evident, the Outline argued that the debate on unity must also include constitutional and legal issues. For various reasons, however, Faith and Order was not in a position to follow up this enquiry.

Comparing the existing church legislations of the Orthodox, Roman Catholic, Lutheran, Reformed and Anglican churches shows a great variety among them in both contents and level of authority. The present study describes the characteristics of these church legislations and suggests that their variety is primarily due to the particular historical contexts in which they emerged. Further sharpening the divergences was the fact that several of these were also a reaction against existing legal models. The confessions of faith of various churches underlined their specificity, thus transplanting the differences into the domain of the faith, thereby becoming sources of church legislations to the extent that they contributed to the creation of specific life-styles.

The establishment of the World Council of Churches (Amsterdam 1948) consolidated a process that aimed to diminish church divisions or, to use the words of the 1974 Outline, to bring churches closer to one another. Bilateral and multilateral dialogues have helped to shape a fellowship of churches, a new international community of believing Christians. This new constellation has not yet received a legal configuration, nor has the juridical position of the WCC within this new international entity been translated into legal forms.

While the Ten Commandments are generally accepted by all Christians, the application of their inherent laws to concrete situations creates difficulties and divisions. An analysis of ethical and moral issues shows that the different theological heritages are at the origin of these divergences. Dialogues between the churches and the development of public and international law may contribute to the disappearance of the variety in this area as well.

For the churches of the Reformation, the Barmen Synod of the Confessing Church in Germany in 1934 stimulated serious reflection on the nature of their church laws; and after the second world war church legislation became a recognized discipline. The legislation of interior church life was related to the faith and its theological sources; demands concerning the ministry and the laity were formulated according to similar patterns. The relationships of the church with the outside world were based on religious freedom and human rights. Wherever possible, the assimilation of civil public laws became common practice. Relations with states and civil authorities followed the official juridical provisions or were regulated in special agreements.

The development of states into democratic nations and the insertion of the churches in this modern society have contributed to developing a political and social atmosphere which is favourable to picking up the 1974 Faith and Order appeal to update church laws in conformity with changed realities, particularly with the progress achieved in the ecumenical movement.

Several other positive signs may encourage resumption of this discussion ecumenically. The Orthodox church is attempting to bring its canon law up to date and to modernize its traditional understanding of church-state relations. The quest for decentralization within the Roman Catholic Church is a likely indication that the monopoly of its canon law and hierarchical structure will give way to increased impact of local churches, each with its specific culture. The *Joint Declaration on the Doctrine of Justification* (1999) has created new theological relationships not only between Rome and the Lutheran church, but also with the other churches of the Reformation. These new relationships have juridical dimensions which demand a legal configuration. The 1999 text from the Anglican-Roman Catholic International Commission, *The Gift of Authority,* aims at close coexistence of the Roman and Anglican churches, with a universal primacy exercised by the bishop of Rome. It is of course too early to give any definitive appreciation of this new theological and ecclesiological model of integrated church authority; indeed its juridical consequences cannot yet be formulated or defined.

The present study goes on to describe the aims of the united and uniting churches. Drawing on a few notable precedents, the united churches movement developed in the 1960s and now includes one-third of the churches represented in the Faith and Order Commission, comprising Reformed, Methodist, Baptist and Episcopalian churches. These churches emphasize not their confessionalism and historical heritage, but rather the ideal of undivided churches. They unite to achieve organic and structural oneness and mutual accountability as one community, while recognizing their theological and institutional diversity.

The 1974 Outline did not aim at establishing one uniform juridical pattern, and no single legal model exists. The dynamism of the ecumenical movement, manifest in its recent developments, may well contribute important elements to the update proposed in 1974.

—

CHAPTER 1

Ecumenism, Ecclesiology and Church Law

General Principles

The old saying that "law follows life" is perhaps more appropriate today than ever before. While changes in the world come ever more rapidly, legislation increasingly lags behind. This is equally true in the area of church law, which still lives with the legacy of Thomas Aquinas, whose vision of the world was influenced by Plato and Aristotle. This vision was a static one – the more static, the more perfect – also with regard to people and their life in society.

Among the Romans, this vision of the world was reflected in the concept of law. The definition of Aquinas – "Law is some kind of ordinance of reason for the sake of common good promulgated by the person who is in charge of the community"[1] – created a climate in which any change appeared as imperfection; and this greatly influenced theologians and church lawyers. Evolution was not readily understood, and development was not assessed in a positive way. The legal structures and juridical status of churches suffered seriously from this "ultra-conservative" identification of immobility with perfection, reflected in the axiom *mutatio legis odiosa est:* "change of law is odious".

Church legislation, its norms, laws and rules generally have an ahistorical character: by their very nature they are meant to remain unaltered. But the world of the believers, which church legislation is intended to influence, develops at a staggering pace, bypassing church laws. Communities of believers and congregations are living bodies. They are mobile: they grow, change and develop. The rapid changes to which humanity is subject also affect churches. To remain credible, the churches need juridical structures and laws which balance stability and openness to change.

The definition of law formulated by Aquinas deals with the abstract essence of law, not with its true function. It is silent about the *existential* dimension of law. The "essential" definition stops with the promulgation of law, not taking account of the fact that life means both continuity and change. Essentially speaking, law is like a snapshot which immortalizes an event and turns it into a static reality. It is closed to new phases of life, to new experiences.

The notion of law as a liberating force is totally absent. No wonder then that attempts are being made to formulate a more dynamic definition of law. The definition proposed by the Catholic canon lawyer Ladislas Örsy is an example: "Law is a norm of action promulgated by a legitimate authority which leads and prompts the community to the appropriation of a value."[2] By considering law as the beginning of a process, this definition understands it as a dynamic instrument of life and growth, prompting the community to look for positive values.

1. Canon law or church order?

In the 16th century, Luther and Calvin replaced the term "church law" by "church order". In doing so, they were reacting against the very nature of Roman Catholic canon law, which had become the dominant legal instrument guiding both church and society and served as the ideological foundation of the entire mediaeval order. The Reformers opposed the legal system of the Catholic Church on theological grounds, since it had grown into the dominant power structure, claiming to base its authority on divine law. Christ was presented as the supreme legislator who had delegated his power, including legislative power, to the bishop of Rome, who was head and absolute primate of the church *de iure divino* – by virtue of divine law. Over the centuries the claims of the popes to full power over spiritual matters had been extended to secular matters.

Luther firmly refused to accept that the salvation of the Christian depends not only on God but also on the bishop of Rome as formulated by canon law. He considered the claim that the pope's authority was based on divine law as sheer arrogance and abuse. Canon law should be considered as a human invention. Luther thought that gospel and law are opposed entities, since law can never legalize faith. Church order should primarily serve church communities in their internal and external organization.

Some non-Catholic churches maintained the term "canon law" or "church law" without claiming (as Rome continued to do) divine origins for its authority and contents. In several Protestant churches, the concept of church order gave way to church law and church legislation under the influence of church law as an independent science in the 19th and 20th centuries. However, many churches, especially of the Reformed tradition still prefer church order or, in North America, "church polity".

Catholic theologians and canon lawyers have also expressed difficulties with the term canon law. The Second Vatican Council – before dealing with the hierarchical structure of the church, the episcopate and the primacy of the bishop of Rome – defined the church first of all as "the people of God", that is, the community of believers. Consequently, canon lawyers made a distinction between the community of faith and the hierarchical institution, the visible society governed by law. However, the new Code of Canon Law (1983) did not take adequate account of this distinction, and it continued to use the traditional image of the church as an institution described and defined in juridical terms, which is to be understood as a legally "perfect society". According to the new trend among Catholic canon lawyers, this institution is structured by a "theologized" hierarchical power of jurisdiction.

The late Peter Huizing, a well-known Jesuit canon lawyer, proposed – like the Reformers – to refer to "church order" rather than to canon law or church law. He and several other canon lawyers argued that a theology of Christ as the supreme legislator of the church could not be legislated by a true church order. The human relationship with God in faith cannot be mediated or legally regulated either by the pope or by the magisterium. To make binding a legislation of the faith is contrary to the free action of God's grace and to the nature of faith as a human response to the divine calling. Divine law framed in legal terms and a christological over-emphasis of hierarchical and papal authority in law and forms of government run counter to the understanding of the church as community of faith. Church order in turn should be responsible for the internal and external legal norms and laws of the church as a hierarchical institution in the form of a "perfect society".[3]

2. Church law and ecclesiology

In the strict sense, church law is not a *constitutive*, but a "consecutive" and "regulative" element of the reality of a church. Theologically, the constitutive foundation of a church is its ecclesiology, its self-understanding of its relationship to the Trinity and to God's action with regard to humanity and creation. Traditionally, the Roman Catholic Church and the Orthodox churches have adhered to these theological convictions. The Church of England has from its beginning followed similar concepts.

Lutheran and Reformed ecclesiology evolved differently. Their real concern for an ecclesiology of their own developed in the course of the centuries. Not until the early 19th century, under the influence of loosened ties with civil authorities, did they begin to have their own system and form. Only at the end of the 19th century and the beginning of the

20th century did the relationships between scripture, the churches' confessions of faith (*Bekenntnisse*) and their system of church law become the object of serious research and study. In the Protestant churches the Apostles' Creed and the Nicene Creed as ancient, traditional expressions of the Christian faith were complemented by a number of confessions of faith which focused on particular doctrinal elements of the Reformation and brought out the specificity of these churches.

The Barmen Synod of the Confessing Church in Germany elaborated several texts of juridical and theological relevance. On 31 May 1934 the Synod issued a "Statement on the Legal Position of the German Evangelical Church". The following days saw the preparation of the "Theological Statement on the Present Condition of the German Evangelical Church". According to the former statement, "in the church a separation of the external legal order from the confession is not possible". The church lawyer Dr Friedler declared at the Synod that "the external juridical order of the church should be at the service of the proclamation of the word, the external order must be tested ever anew by the confession of faith, and on no level of legal church life can juridical questions be solved without relation to the church's confession".[4] Swiss theologian Karl Barth, who participated actively in the Barmen Synod, also saw a close relationship between a church's legal order and its confession. The church's confession should be at the root of its legislation: "church law is a confessing order". Church legislation is thus *sui generis,* utterly different from the legislation of any other society. And Barth added: "The church order or church law is part of the confessing response of the believers to the action of God and Christ in Word and Sacrament."[5]

The Barmen Synod and Barth's position had a positive influence on the ecclesiological thinking of the Protestant churches. The conviction that church order or church law should be conceived and elaborated from the mission of the church – and particularly from the specific faith confession of the churches – came to be generally accepted. Scripture and faith confession must have a normative role in church legislation.

3. Ecumenism and church law

When the ecumenical movement and, from 1948 onwards, the World Council of Churches began slowly but surely to break the isolation of the churches from each other and to create a network of authentic relationships, the legal systems of the individual churches came under pressure. Not only the Protestant churches but also the Roman Catholic, Orthodox and Anglican churches had to cope with this new reality.

Theologians and particularly church lawyers gradually became aware that the growing ecumenical network should also be formulated in legal terms. The many bilateral and multilateral dialogues not only have theological and ecclesiological implications; they also have a juridical dimension, which requires a legal expression. The same is true of inter-church and inter-confessional agreements which call for action by legally authorized representatives of the churches involved. At the sacramental level, it is recognized that common baptism creates juridical rights and duties. There is also the question of hospitality or *communio in spiritualibus*, including the proclamation of the word and participation in the eucharist, agreed upon by various churches. There are, however, no specific juridical norms regulating these. The process towards theological convergences on doctrinal issues such as justification, church, sacraments and ministry leaves the door open for a common ecclesiological understanding, but this has not yet found a translation into juridical terms.

Setting up an ecumenical legal system which corresponds to this new reality is certainly not the task of a few individual theologians and church lawyers. The formulation of juridical norms and laws covering new theological and ecclesiological realities should be the result of convergences and consent involving as many churches as possible.

A first attempt to start such a process was in fact made by the WCC Commission on Faith and Order more than 35 years ago. At its meeting in Aarhus, Denmark, in 1964, Faith and Order launched a study on "Spirit, Order and Institution". A concluding report was presented to the Commission meeting in Louvain, Belgium, in 1971. The study was not pursued, mainly because of lack of funds, but the Commission at its meeting in Accra, Ghana, in 1974 approved a more limited attempt to take up "the role of constitutional matters (church law) in efforts towards the visible unity of the church". An Outline for a study of "The Ecumenical Movement and Church Law" was accepted; however, when the Commission met in Bangalore in 1978, the director reported that "not much progress has been made on this proposal and, given the limited resources available to the Commission, the study will probably never get very far". The same year Faith and Order and the Ecumenical Institute of Bossey held a joint consultation which produced a report, *Church and State: Opening a New Ecumenical Discussion*. But as former Faith and Order director Günther Gassmann wrote in 1993:

> Limited financial and personnel resources and, consequently, the need to concentrate on a few major studies have prevented Faith and Order from implementing these initiatives in the areas of institution, church law and church and state. But questions and conflicts in these areas have accompanied the ecumenical movement ever since, which confirms the foresight of those earlier initiatives and the need to take them up once again.[6]

The 1974 Outline is still relevant in the sense that the problems it addresses remain unresolved after 25 years. It begins by noting that sooner or later the ecumenical quest for "the visible unity of the church in the one eucharistic fellowship" will raise issues of church law. While "the churches differ in their legal order and in their constitution", so far "the ecumenical discussion on the unity of the church has almost exclusively concentrated on issues of doctrine and worship as the most obvious causes for the division of the church... With the advance of the ecumenical movement, the debate will need to include more and more constitutional and legal issues." Progress towards the unity of the church inevitably raises the question of how the churches' different legal orders can be brought closer to one another. Therefore, "if the churches are to go beyond the present state of their divisions, the ecumenical movement needs to provide them with some help in dealing with the legal issues arising from their mutual encounter".

While it is difficult to visualize what will be the legal structure when the ultimate goal of the ecumenical movement, the unity of the church, has been realized, the churches committed to this quest should, in progressing towards this ultimate goal, "try to work out solutions which will further or at least not hinder the process of convergence towards unity which has already started". To achieve this, the Outline suggests that instead of leaving these questions to individual experts or to the individual churches,

> the ecumenical movement and especially its Commission on Faith and Order make a conscious effort to help member churches... by engaging in a serious study of the legal aspects of inter-church cooperation and eventual church union. For even if the ultimate goal may still seem very distant, there are at present several features in the progress of the ecumenical movement which make it urgent to take up these kinds of questions within the framework of the Faith and Order Commission.

The Outline mentions several factors which point to a changed or changing legal situation within the ecumenical movement:

a. Growing ecumenical fellowship has induced churches to abolish mutual condemnations or rules against inter-church contacts or cooperation, raising the question of the present validity of such statements and rules.

b. New structures and regulations, not foreseen in the traditional legal system of the churches, have arisen out of ecumenical fellowship, such as new financial systems and representative systems which in the past did not need to be juridically legitimized.

c. Agreements reached in ecumenical dialogue call for juridical implementation. This may imply changes in the churches' constitutions

(*Kirchenverfassung*) – for example, references to confessions of faith –
or changes in their discipline – for example, rules for ordination, inter-
celebration and inter-communion.

d. When dialogue leads to closer collaboration, new ecumenical
structures often come into being. What is their juridical significance?
Can the competence of decision-making of the church be transferred to
such "para-constitutional" bodies?

e. Implementation of ecumenical agreements and common action at
the international level require that churches have freedom of decision-
making and action. How far are churches – especially those in close relationship with a state – free to decide as a church and to dispose of their
resources in order to give priority to solidarity with other churches?

The ecumenical significance of church law becomes more evident in
reflecting on a range of underlying issues. Besides a peculiar theological
position, a specific confessional allegiance and an institutional history,
every church or Christian community has a concrete social and legal
form. It has an inner structure of its own and occupies a "social space"
acknowledged by the larger political and civil society. Furthermore,
every Christian community is fundamentally related, in both its internal
legal structure and its external legal form, to its understanding of the
gospel. How these elements are related to one another and how churches
and Christian communities assess their gospel mission differ from one
situation to the next, from one place to the another.

Many of these differences are rooted in different confessional traditions. Indeed, the Outline observes, it can be argued

> that the confessional heritage persists most powerfully in the different ways in
> which the churches are constituted and perpetuate the inherited juridical order.
> The differences concern not only the actual juridical order which the churches
> have, but also the general orientation by which their legislation is inspired.

Moreover, inter-church relationships often depend on the place and
the role of a church within a specific civil society or state. Problems may
arise when civil authorities and church leaders have different views on
the purpose of church structures, or when a church finds itself in oppo-
sition to an officially backed state religion. In the present rapidly changing world, the roles open to churches either create new opportunities or
become increasingly outdated.

> In such a fluid situation, we urgently need to study the range of possibilities
> open to the church in different circumstances and different parts of the world.
> A comparative study, or typology, of existing and emerging forms of the
> church in legal perspective would help us. The relation of such structures to
> theological understanding, their practical strengths and weaknesses, their
> kinds of responsiveness to ecumenical responsibility, could all be considered.

The Outline suggests that four fundamental questions might underlie such a comparative survey:

1. How do the different churches conceive the relation between the notion of "the people of God" theologically considered and "the people of God" juridically embodied? Is this a question of the relation of church law to civil law, a question of the foundations of law as such, a matter of grace and law related, or grace and law opposed? Or must the issue be formulated in some other way?

2. How do different churches understand the content, style and functioning of their internal legal systems? How is the law applied? What role does ecumenical commitment now play in these written and unwritten codes? What issues are at stake as the different churches reconsider and reformulate their canons, constitutions, by-laws and guidelines?

3. Are there common convictions among the churches about what sorts of relation to the civil community best make for faithfulness to the gospel and ecumenical responsibility to each other? Is there a trend towards "disestablishment" or is the tendency now the opposite? Is there any agreement about what "establishment" and "disestablishment" mean? Do the churches advocate the notion of the "secular state" and do they agree what this means?

4. What do the churches see as the critical issues affecting their integrity and identity in modern societies? Do they feel that circumstances tend to force a certain identity on them? Do they feel free to redefine and re-express their identity as insight and circumstances demand? Can they affirm, in concrete terms, an ecumenical identity – and how?

The Outline goes on to address the implications of the ecumenical movement for the churches' legal systems. Noting that church legislation lags far behind the theological and ecclesiological ecumenical results, it asks how far the churches' legal texts reflect ecumenical progress on such practical issues as relations with Christians of other churches (mixed marriages, common worship), the role of the whole people of God in the decision-making processes of the churches, the freedom of action required if the churches are to participate effectively in the universal fellowship of all churches (church-state relations, synodal structures) and representation (who speaks for the church in dialogue and ecumenical assemblies, and who is entitled to do so?).

Finally, the Outline asks how the questions it formulates should be put to the churches. The first aim is to find out the extent to which the legal framework of the churches has the flexibility required in order for them fully to discharge their responsibility in worship, witness and service on the ecumenical level, both national and international. A method should be devised to overcome the general resistance of churches to changing their legislation, allowing it to catch up with today's ecumenical reality. To start the process of legal updating, the Outline recommends that the Faith and Order Commission establish a small committee of theologians and legal, administrative and sociological experts to produce a working paper to circulate among the churches.

4. Church law and the gospel

Updating the churches' legal systems in response to the changed reality created by the ecumenical movement is not a solely juridical matter; indeed, it is first and foremost a theological and spiritual issue. As Karl Barth says, church order or church law is part of the believer's confessing response to the action of God and Christ in word and sacrament. The common mission of all Christian churches is to proclaim God's relationship with creation and loving concern for humankind, expressed most clearly in the life, death and resurrection of Jesus Christ and in the outpouring of the Holy Spirit. The churches' task is also to guide believers in matters of faith and consequently in their daily life.

Historically speaking, the great merit of the 16th-century Reformers, especially Luther and Calvin, was to have placed their "new ideas" on justification by God alone at the very heart of the Christian faith. They emphasized that Christian life in all its aspects, both personal and ecclesial, must be considered in the light of God's freely given saving grace. The Christian must rely totally on God's justifying and sanctifying action, not on personal works or presumed merits. At the same time, the Reformers stressed the importance of Scripture as the primary source of Christian faith and life.

Scripture is thus the fundamental source and guideline for church order and church law and its adaptation to present ecumenical realities. Scripture has a threefold function in this context, according to Joachim Mehlhausen, professor of church law at Tübingen University:

1. it is *corrective,* in the sense that what is contrary to Scripture can never become a guideline of church law;
2. it is *authoritative,* in the sense that what is in agreement with Scripture is determinative for church law; Scripture in this sense legitimates church law;
3. it is *normative*, in the sense that it provides the example that must be followed in the formulation of church law.[7]

Besides Scripture, confessions of faith also constitute a source of Christian church law. While Scripture is considered the *norma normans*, several confessions which date back to the ancient times of the Christian church are seen as the second norm, *norma normata,* for church law. In one way or another, the Apostles' Creed, the Niceno-Constantinopolitan Creed and the Athanasian Creed enjoy high respect in all Christian churches to the present day.

Following the teaching of the Reformers, several confessions of faith were written to formulate both common elements of the Reformation and areas of divergence marking the specific identity of the different communities and churches that had emerged. Mehlhausen says in this connection:

> With regard to the theological foundation of the nature of the church, Scriptures and confessions of faith were considered as constitutive. There never was any doubt that Scriptures and confessions of faith were of fundamental importance for the churches of the Reformation and their legal systems, but for centuries the specific relationships between church law, Scriptures and confessions of faith were not further studied and explained.[8]

Luther and Calvin differed on the relation between Scripture and law. As a jurist himself, Calvin's ideas were partly shaped by his own respect for the law. He considered the Hebrew Scriptures and the New Testament as one unity. God's covenant with Israel finds its extension in the New Testament and culminates in Jesus Christ. The covenant becomes the promise given to the reborn, the elect. In the Torah, the covenant is manifest not only in the Decalogue but also in the prescriptions concerning temple service and worship revealed to Moses and the prophets. In the New Testament, both law and gospel manifest the covenant in Christ. Calvin believes that the gospel not only contains the word of God, but also includes the witness of God's mercy and lovingkindness.

In the Bible as a whole, law has a disciplinary function. It is to be understood in the light of the covenant and as such it has its "third and principal use" (*tertius usus legis*).[9] "Also according to Calvin the gospel has the primary role, but the gospel in a broader sense conceals the intimate unity of the law and the teaching of Christ."[10]

Calvin sees in the law the expression of the need to do God's will. For both Luther and Calvin justification is the beginning of rebirth in Christ and a process of growth of the "new person". While totally relying on God's mercy, fear of judgment leads to a life in obedience to divine law and church discipline. As a result of Calvin's emphasis on discipline as a necessary element of church order or church law, it became one of the "marks" of the Reformed churches.

In his *Catechism of the Church of Geneva* (1542) Calvin writes that "although we shall never satisfy the law in this earthly pilgrimage of ours, yet we shall not consider it to be superfluous, because it demands such strict perfection from us. For it shows us the mark at which we ought to aim and the goal to which we must strive; that each of us... may try to conform his life to the highest rectitude, and by assiduous care make more and more progress."[11] God "forms new minds and new hearts in us, so that of ourselves we may wish nothing, but rather that his Spirit rule our desires, so that they may have complete agreement with God".[12]

Hence, according to Calvin and Luther, justification stands at the beginning of a process of "sanctification" towards spiritual perfection or holiness. In other Christian churches as well, perfection and holiness in obedience to the gospel are clearly considered the fundamental elements of Christian faith and life. For this reason, the adaptation and updating of the churches' legal systems is related not only to the juridical realm but also to the domains of theology and spirituality.

NOTES

1 *Summa Theologiae*, I-II, q. 90, ad.1-4.

2 Ladislas Örsy, *Theology and Canon Law: New Horizons for Legislation and Interpretation*, Collegeville MN, The Liturgical Press, 1992, p.92.

3 Karl-Christoph Kuhn, "Church Order instead of Church Law", in *Concilium*, 5, 1996, pp.29-39.

4 Quoted by Albert Stein, in *"Herrschaft Christi und geschwisterliche Gemeinde"*, in Gerhard Rau, Hans-Richard Reuter, Klaus Schlaich, eds, *Das Recht der Kirche*, Gütersloh, Chr. Kaiser, 1995, Vol. 2, p.286.

5 K. Barth, *Die Kirchliche Dogmatik, IV/3*, 1. Hälfte, Zollikon-Zurich, 1959, pp.40ff.

6 Günther Gassman, ed., *Documentary History of Faith and Order 1963-1993*, Geneva, WCC Publications, 1993, p.207, cf. pp.283-88.

7 Joachim Mehlhausen, "Kirchenverfassung und Kirchengesetz", in *Das Recht der Kirche*, Vol. 1, pp. 426f.

8 *Ibid.*, p.446.

9 John Calvin, *Institutes of the Christian Religion*, II.7.12.

10 Ulrich H.J. Körtner, *Reformiert und Oekumenisch: Brennpunkte reformierter Theologie in Geschichte und Gegenwart*, Innsbruck and Vienna, Tyrolia-Verlag, 1998, pp.65-69.

11 English text in J.K.S. Reid, ed., *Calvin: Theological Treatises*, Philadelphia, Westminster, 1954, p.118.

12 *Ibid.*, p.125.

CHAPTER 2

Church Legislations: Characteristics

Updating church legislation, as the 1974 Faith and Order Outline proposes, is no easy task, in part because of the great variety of contents, forms and authority which a comparative study of the various legislations reveals.

1. The Orthodox church

The canon law of the Orthodox church is an expression of the Orthodox ecclesiology and, more specifically, of Orthodox Tradition. The authority and impact of Tradition are based on Holy Scripture and the patristic teaching of the revelation of the Holy Trinity. Furthermore, Tradition is constituted by the doctrine and teaching found in the official reports of the first seven ecumenical councils, from the First Council of Nicea (325) to the Second Council of Nicea (787). Both clergy and laity are responsible for the preservation of this authentic and genuine Tradition.

Nicea I and subsequent Councils elaborated canons to provide the church with disciplinary measures. Local synods, several fathers of the patristic era and some individual bishops of the first centuries provided the material for other canons. All were brought together in a collection which constituted the first and major Orthodox canon law. This was considered an authentic interpretation of Tradition, to be used for practical situations in the daily life of the church and the Christian behaviour of its members. Over the centuries authentic interpretations and commentaries were added. Besides the universal canon law, the patriarchates and autocephalous local churches worked out collections of their own church laws, whose relative authority depended on a synod or an individual member of the patriarchal or metropolitan hierarchy. Some Orthodox theologians feel that the growing importance of the Russian Orthodox Church and growing nationalistic trends have increasingly made the Orthodox church an aggregation of almost totally independent national churches, which are affected by religious nationalism, though a council in Constantinople in 1872 condemned as heretical "the formation of particular churches which exclusively receive members of the same nation, excluding those of other nationalities".[1]

Although the first systematic collection of canons appeared in the 12th century, not until 1800 did the first edition of the *Pedalion* ("Rudder") appear in Greek, providing the text of each canon, followed by a paraphrase in modern Greek and a commentary, often based on Byzantine canonists. Juridical and liturgical canons are often interpreted at length. The *Pedalion* received official approval of the patriarch of Constantinople. For a long time, the Orthodox Slavs simply translated and reproduced texts of Byzantine commentators, but in the 19th century Slavic canonists initiated their own canonical studies which, generally speaking, were more historical than doctrinal.

An English version of the *Pedalion* was published in 1957.[2] It begins with the "Original Creed" as formulated by the early Ecumenical Councils. An extensive editorial foreword contains explanatory notes on "the moral belief in the divine law" and on the infallibility of the books of the Bible and of the first seven Ecumenical Councils concerning dogma and doctrine. A long essay deals with the faults and heretical aberrations of the Church of Rome, which led to the schism of the 11th century.

The *Pedalion* is a valuable witness to the first centuries of Orthodox church life and Christian behaviour, and as such canon law belongs to the Orthodox Tradition. Canon law has become a guide or orientation, a reference point and a source of information for Orthodox church organization and discipline and for Christian moral behaviour. In Orthodox discussions of the applicability of Orthodox canon law and its canons to today's realities, viewpoints diverge widely. While some would stick to the letter of the canons and oppose any idea of updating, others deny the relevance of the entire body of canons as it presently stands; still others would consider the canons, as a juridical interpretation of the dogmas for a particular moment of the church's historical existence, to be pastoral guidelines and models on which to base subsequent church legislation.

In this connection the concept of economy *(oikonomia)* as a particular characteristic of Orthodox church legislation is relevant. The purpose of Orthodox church law is the spiritual perfection or holiness of the members of the church. The spirit of love as a means to attain perfection or holiness also prevails in the application of church law. In the words of Lewis Patsavos, "the abolition of the letter of the law by the spirit of the law has led to the institution of economy, exercised in non-essential matters. Through economy, which is always an exception to the general rule, the legal consequences following the violation of a law are lifted."[3]

Economy, granted by a competent ecclesiastical authority, has been applied throughout the history of the Orthodox church. It can be applied as an exception to a law which has no universal status, and when it is deemed spiritually beneficial. Since church law is characterized in the eyes of Orthodox faithful by grace and love, economy should be marked by compassion, sensitivity and forgiveness. Once applied, the normative character of the law is restored. Economy is almost always a matter of conscience; thus, a spiritual counsellor is entrusted with the authority to exercise it in accordance with his personal judgment. The spiritual welfare of the believer should be the decisive criterion. Seen in this perspective, the Orthodox tradition does not consider canon law to be of primary importance. Over of the centuries it was partially replaced by legislations of the autocephalous churches.

2. The Roman Catholic Church

The Code of Canon Law promulgated by Pope John Paul II in 1983 is first and foremost a collection of canons, canonical norms, rules and prescriptions which officially and authoritatively regulate the entire life of the Roman Catholic Church (RCC) at all levels. It comprises all of the juridical rules for institutional ecclesiology, the juridical and hierarchical structures of the Roman Catholic Church as a visible institution and the functions of the various authorities concerning internal and external relationships, including those with state authorities. It also provides norms, laws and prescriptions for the conduct of life of all members of the church, including disciplinary rules and juridical measures in cases of transgression. Its status can be compared to that of the constitution of a state and its codes of civil and penal laws. The Code of Canon Law is based on the concept of a "perfect society", in analogy with secular states. It represents the deposit of Catholic ecclesiology, of the primacy of the Roman pontiff and of the binding doctrinal statements issued by him and the magisterium.

The Code of Canon Law can be expressed in the following legal terms:

1. Alongside, above and independently from the legal systems of secular states, the Roman Catholic Church forms a universal, sovereign, autonomous religious order.

2. This legal order is based on the universal legal power of the pope over the entire Roman Catholic Church, represented in dioceses by bishops appointed by him for the implementation of his government.

3. In matters of faith the lower clergy and the laity are passive subjects of the hierarchy. No theological *locus* of the *sensus fidelium* is taken into account.

The Code of Canon Law makes the following distinction: "Among the Christian faithful by divine institution there exist in the Church sacred ministers, who are also called clerics in law, and other Christian faithful, who are also called laity" (Canon 207).[4] Canon 274 stipulates that "only clerics can obtain those offices for whose exercise there is required the power of orders or the power of ecclesiastical governance".

The Apostolic Constitution through which the pope promulgated the Code of 1983 emphasizes its newness, in that it seeks to translate into canonical language the teaching and ecclesiology of the Second Vatican Council. The Code indeed follows the Council's Dogmatic Constitution on the Church (*Lumen Gentium*) – in which, however, the chapter on "The Hierarchical Structure of the Church" was preceded by a chapter on "The People of God".

The Apostolic Constitution emphasizes that the commitment of the Roman Catholic Church to ecumenism is a new element in the 1983 Code. The Apostolic See and the College of Bishops have the mandate to "promote and direct the participation of Catholics in the ecumenical movement" (Canon 755,1). Bishops and bishops' conferences are required "to issue practical norms for the needs and opportunities presented by diverse circumstances in the light of prescriptions of the supreme Church authority" (755,2). Bishops are asked "to act with kindness and charity towards those who are not in full communion with the Catholic Church, fostering ecumenism as it is understood by the Church" (383,3).

According to the chapter on the people of God,

> The Christian faithful are those who, inasmuch as they have been incorporated in Christ through baptism, have been constituted as the people of God...; they are called to exercise the mission which God has entrusted to the Church to fulfill in the world... This Church, constituted and organized as a society in this world, subsists in the Catholic Church, governed by the successor of Peter and the bishops in communion with him (Canon 204,1,2).

This text picks up the description given in *Lumen Gentium,* whose final version used the words "subsists in" rather than the wording of earlier drafts, which stated that "the unique Church of Christ *is* the Catholic Church".[5] This modification was introduced to make the text correspond better to statements in other documents of the Council that ecclesial elements can be found outside the Catholic Church. However, according to authoritative interpretations of *Lumen Gentium* such as *Mysterium Ecclesiae,* issued in 1973 by the Congregation for the Doctrine of the Faith, the expression "subsists in" should be understood as follows: "The Catholic Church is the unique Church of Christ."[6]

The theology of the 1983 Code of Canon Law begins from the supposition that the relation between law and grace is not contradictory. The new law as introduced by Christ is not constraining because of its legal nature, but in virtue of grace, which belongs fundamentally to its essence. In the words of Thomas Aquinas, "the new law is the very grace (or the presence of the Holy Spirit) that is given to the Christian faithful."[7] It follows that the law, which does not as such produce salvation, is not only an exterior result of grace, but also a true requisite of salvation, although law comes about with the help of grace. According to Catholic theology, the incarnation of Christ is a principle that pervades all domains of the economy of salvation: grace, sacraments and church. Thus "canon law is not only a sociological product based on the Bible, but a true development of *ius divinum* in history".[8]

From the time of the *Decretum Gratiani* (1140), *ius divinum* (divine law) in the Roman Catholic Church has been related to divine origin. Catholic ecclesiology affirms that throughout the centuries the church is guided and inspired by its Lord. The Spirit is actively concerned with the requirements of history as these appear in ecclesial life, so that the people of God may remain faithful to its nature and mission. Hence it is necessary to determine whether an issue is not only useful but also necessary to the church, and whether it can be related to revelation and thus willed by God. This search for the will of God in the light of the Scriptures is an essential element of Catholic theology: there where God's will can be uncovered, the issues concerned are *de iure divino*, because they represent the will of God. In this sense, Canadian theologian J.-M. Tillard writes, "the primacy of the bishop of Rome has appeared as a principle of unity laid down by God, even with regard to the institution of the Church to maintain the communion of faith, the witness and mission of all the Churches dispersed throughout the entire world."[9]

The Code of Canon Law is explicit about the place and authority of the bishop of Rome:

> The bishop of the Church of Rome, in whom resides the office given in a special way by the Lord to Peter, first of the Apostles, and to be transmitted to his successors, is head of the College of Bishops, the Vicar of Christ and Pastor of the universal Church on earth; he therefore, in virtue of his office, enjoys supreme, full, immediate and universal ordinary power in the Church, which he can always freely exercise (Canon 331).
>
> The Roman Pontiff, by virtue of his office, not only has power in the universal Church, but also possesses a primacy of ordinary power over all particular churches and groupings of churches. The Roman Pontiff, in fulfilling the office of the supreme pastor of the church, is always united in communion with the other bishops and with the universal Church; however, he has the right, according to the needs of the Church, to determine the manner, either

personal or collegial, of exercising this function. There is neither appeal nor recourse against a decision or decree of the Roman Pontiff (Canon 333).

The pope governs the Roman Catholic Church with the help of the Roman Curia: "The Supreme Pontiff usually conducts the business of the universal Church by means of the Roman Curia, which fulfills its duty in his name and by his authority for the good and the service of the churches" (Canon 360). However, there is no canon defining the authority of the departments of the Roman Curia when these deal with diocesan bishops. According to Canon 362, the Roman pontiff has the "independent" right to appoint his own legates to particular churches, to states and public authorities. Canon 365 describes the duties of the papal representatives to states: to promote relations with the Apostolic See and the pope as sovereign of the Vatican Papal State, and to oversee the drafting and implementation of concordats and other agreements.

In 1870, the First Vatican Council declared, in Canon 203:

> If anyone says that the blessed Apostle Peter was not constituted by Christ the Lord as the Prince of all the Apostles and the visible head of the whole Church militant, or that he received immediately and directly from Jesus Christ our Lord only a primacy of honour and not a true and proper primacy of jurisdiction: let him be anathema. If anyone says that it is not according to the institution of Christ our Lord himself, that is, *de iure divino*, by divine law, that St Peter has perpetual successors in the primacy over the whole Church; or if anyone says that the Roman Pontiff is not the successor of St Peter in the same primacy: let him be anathema.[10]

The Second Vatican Council said, in its Dogmatic Constitution on the Church, that

> Jesus Christ... set up the holy Church by entrusting the apostles with their mission... He willed that their successors, the bishops namely, should be the shepherds in his Church until the end of the world. In order that the episcopate itself, however, might be one and undivided he put Peter at the head of the other apostles, and in him he set up a lasting and visible source and foundation of the unity both of faith and of communion. This teaching concerning the institution, the permanence, the nature and import of the sacred primacy of the Roman Pontiff and his infallible teaching office, the sacred synod proposes anew to be firmly believed by all the faithful.[11]

Especially since the Second Vatican Council, theologians have studied in depth the ecclesiological consequences of the status of the bishop of Rome and the legal expression "by divine law". The late bishop of Lugano, canonist Eugenio Corecco, concluded that this juridical formula was inserted into official documents concerning papal primacy at the time of the Reformation. German theologian Karl Rahner called for critical theological reflection on the historical development of the papacy. Tillard, who has extensively studied the local church and the long syn-odal tradition, underscores the consequences of the present form of the papacy for an "ecumenical synodal dynamism".[12] In his book on author-ity in the Roman Catholic Church, Edward Schillebeeckx argues that its present form is the result of historical developments. According to Schillebeeckx, the heart of the matter in all official Roman Catholic documents is:

> Democratic government harms subjection to God's revelation. Why? Such an argument is in my view a false argument, which has as its tacit ideology the view that the authority in power (because guided by the Holy Spirit) is always right; it does not need to be unnecessarily hindered in its actions by contribu-tions from below... But the supposedly non-democratic structure of the Church is in no way rooted in the nature of the Church, but can only be defended with a straight reference to the actual contingent history of this Church, which until recently moved in non-democratic civil societies and then to a large degree took over the non-democratic forms of governments of the surrounding social and cultural milieu... The rejection by the official Church of the possibility of a democratically governed community of faith in fact has nothing to do with subjection to the word of God, which is under no one's sovereign control, not that of the community of faith, nor that of the hierarchy, whereas on the offi-cial side constantly renewed subjection to the word of God is and was the only argument against the democratic exercising of authority in the Church.[13]

3. The Lutheran and Reformed churches

The era of the Reformation coincided with the transition from the uniform spiritual and temporal *Corpus Christianorum* of the Middle Ages to a new constellation of pre-modern territorial states. Canon law dominated and regulated both the public and the private order, becoming the unique legal framework for church and civil society alike. On the ter-ritorial level, bishops had become important rulers – princes with both spiritual and temporal authority and power. When the bishop-princes became increasingly independent, canon law remained the primary legal source.

Martin Luther's attitude towards canon law was directly related to the central theological conviction expressed in his doctrine of justifica-tion. In connection with this doctrine, Luther distinguished the "hidden or spiritual church" (*ecclesia abscondita, seu spiritualis*) from the visi-ble church on earth, formulating a concept of the church as the exclusive gathering of those who believe in Christ. He was convinced that canon law, by abusing the term "spiritual law", had led Christianity "to fatal perdition".[14] Spiritual law and human law are not applicable to spiritual Christianity and the *ecclesia abscondita*. The authentic spiritual church has no room for the pope's claim to sovereign power, nor for other church authorities and powers. The pope and the bishops have only the function of vicars or stewards, just as the apostles did.

Luther publicly manifested his break with canon law by burning the papal decretals in Wittenberg on 10 December 1520. At the end of that month he published a refutation of canon law under the title *Why the Books of the Pope and His Disciples are Burned.*15 His principal criticisms are directed at the pope's pretentious position and his primacy in the church, his claim to unlimited jurisdictional power, the fact that he is not accountable to anyone, his standing above the general council and other Christian institutions, his power to enact laws on spiritual and temporal affairs, and the idea that Jesus Christ has given to him – rather than to the entire congregation of believers – the "power of the keys", so that the salvation of Christians depends not only on God but also on the pope. In Luther's view, canon law turns the pope into a "God on earth", to whom not only Scripture but even Christ is subordinated.16

While Luther reproaches those who claim that canon law is necessary for salvation and binding on the human conscience, he does not reject it in its entirety and indeed accepts it insofar as it serves salvation. His main concern is with its abuse by the popes in their thirst for power.17 But he totally refuses the claim that the authority of canon law is *de iure divino*, in virtue of divine law, and the concept of papal primacy based on it.

Luther relates the dialectic between law and gospel to divine law and human law. He considers church law, in the sense of divine law, as exclusively related to the *ecclesia spiritualis* and its members, in which the will of God reigns. Church laws made by human persons in the service of the congregation are there to create and maintain order and discipline and hence should rather be called "church *orders*". Nevertheless, an element of divine law remains in the church on earth, namely Scripture and the proclamation of the word.

Luther's collaborator Melanchthon (1497-1560) did not so rigorously limit *ius divinum* to the spiritual church or the *ecclesia abscondita* as did Luther. With Melanchthon began a process of identifying Scripture, the *mandatum Dei* and the proclamation of the word, with *ius divinum*:

> The criterion for *ius divinum* becomes in the course of the centuries increasingly a harmonizing process with Scripture. The distinction between *ius divinum* and *ius humanum* no longer serves the aim of underlining the character of human law in the church.18

The need to base church order or church law on Scripture and confessions of faith became a growing concern in the churches of the Reformation, alongside the struggle to liberate the churches and church laws from the influence of the ruling territorial princes. While Luther had left it to them to draw up church laws, already in the time of Melanchthon the legislation of the congregation was entrusted to the Lutheran bishops. In this way church laws in the churches of the Reformation not only acquired a juridical character, but also received a theological and spiritual dimension.

John Calvin (1509-1564) became acquainted with Luther's theological ideas through the humanists. He tried to formulate a synthesis of Luther's main theses that would be in conformity with his own insights and aspirations and correspond to the needs of the French-speaking world. To understand his convictions about law and its impact on Christian believers, several elements of Calvin's theological thinking must be kept in mind. While the decisive issues for Luther were God as the source of all graces and the justification of sinners, the core of Calvin's convictions was the authority and sovereignty of God and the nothingness of the human person. To God as Creator all glory, reverence, love and fear are owed. As creatures we depend on God's will and have to give him all that pleases him, Calvin wrote in his *Institutes of the Christian Religion.*[19] Calvin's adage *soli Deo gloria* implied a total and decisive separation between God and the human person. The human person and, in fact, all creation are totally corrupted by sin.

Like Luther, Calvin distinguishes between the hidden, invisible church and the visible church on earth. Characteristic for his ecclesiology is the free act of divine election. The elect, illuminated through the power of the Spirit, are called to faith, born again and incorporated into Christ. Only God knows the elect, and it is a presumption on the part of any human person to indicate who is a true member of Christ and who is not.

Calvin's concept of the relations between Scripture and law differs from that of Luther and Melanchthon. As a jurist, Calvin had a profound respect for the law. Furthermore, given the covenant of God with Israel, he considered the Hebrew Scriptures and the New Testament as a unity: the covenant with Israel finds its extension in the New Testament and culminates in Jesus Christ.

Calvin agreed with Luther that the church had seriously abused canon law by giving it authority in virtue of divine law and making it binding on the conscience. Nor, like Luther, did he accept canon law as a means to salvation. Furthermore, he refused to accept the pope's claim to have, *de iure divino*, absolute and supreme authority over spiritual and temporal affairs.[20] His theological convictions left no room for an intermediary between God and the believer. Calvin preferred to speak of *lex divina* rather than *ius divinum. Lex divina* is first of all God's sovereign will, expressed in Scripture and in the human person whose conscience manifests the will of God.

Calvin was convinced that the elect, the reborn, need a law to live in conformity with God's will. In relation to Scripture, law has guiding and disciplinary functions, to be understood in the light of the covenant, which has for the elect the significance of a divine promise. In this respect, law manifested in church order or church law has the primary function of order, discipline and morality.

Calvin saw *ius divinum* in the context of the invisible, spiritual church which is constituted by God's freedom to choose the elect. In this sense, *ius divinum* has nothing to do with church law, which is based on Scripture – wherever possible on its very words. While the spiritual church can in no way be determined by church law, through Scripture church law is related to the spiritual domain. The *lex divina* is a spiritual law. God is spirit; consequently, so is his law. The believer who is inspired by the Spirit fulfills the law of the church through the action of the Spirit.

In the social and political context of the 16th-century Reformation, it became necessary to transfer to new rulers the episcopal oversight (*ius episcopale*) which had made of the bishops not only spiritual leaders with church authority in their diocese, but also temporal governors with civil jurisdiction over their territory. The territories which adhered to the new doctrines were henceforth governed by sovereign rulers or princes. Since they were eminent members of the new communities, they took over the jurisdiction and administrative powers which had formerly belonged to the bishops. They also inherited the *advocatio ecclesiae*, the patronage of the church, which included the duty of defending it against heresies. This juridical foundation gave them the right and the duty to fight the "heresies" and "blasphemies" of the Church of Rome.

The new rulers and princes also had the power of legislation. In this capacity they were responsible for church legislation – and Luther agreed with this principle. From the beginning, however, the conception and the formulation of the texts themselves were in the hands of bishops and theologians. So for example in the territory of Hesse (Germany), the synod was in charge of the church laws from 1526 on. Luther invited theologians to Wittenberg to elaborate a set of norms for church legislation. This was a prelude to future church constitutions (*Kirchenverfassungen*).

Congregations adhering to Calvin's doctrinal and ethical convictions had much looser ties with territorial and local governors. Calvin prescribed that Christians should respect and obey civil authorities, but the internal affairs of the congregations and the formulation of church legislation remained with the consistory.

Historically speaking, it took centuries for the Lutheran churches in Germany and in the Scandinavian countries to liberate themselves from state interference in church life. The influence of territorial rulers and princes was fully legitimated at the Peace of Augsburg (1555) and the Peace of Westphalia (1648), when the juridical formula *cuius regio, illius religio* was introduced. In the 17th and 18th centuries the churches were organically incorporated into the state or the *Land*, thus becoming state churches. From about 1750 through the first world war they were able to administer their own internal affairs, but the state continued to have the right of inspection and supervision of church matters concerning the external order. Between 1919 and 1933 the Lutheran and Reformed churches in Germany, in close collaboration and "union" (and in imitation of the Roman Catholic Church), made agreements with the Weimar Republic which were in effect an expression of church-state separation. The Scandinavian Lutheran churches were at first incorporated into the state, although at the present time the interference of the state in internal church life is limited to a minimum.

Church order and church legislation underwent an important development when the emergence of confessions of faith and catechisms between 1540 and 1650 offered a new source for the formulation of church laws. Whether these new sources were quoted directly or indirectly taken into account, the relation between these doctrinal documents and church laws was so close that confessions and catechisms were henceforth considered to belong to what was meant by the term "church order". From about 1650 onwards, church order was further augmented by the addition of another element, namely church constitution *(Verfassung)*. This contained general norms for the life of the church, administration of the sacraments, proclamation of the word and relations with the state, as well as references to the historical events in the life of the church and broad norms for the moral life of the members. The word "constitution" already indicates the analogy with state legislation and as such constitutes the most important and stable element of the whole church order complex. In general, constitutions are officially approved by local, provincial and national synods.[21]

In the Reformed tradition sets of fundamental Christian rights have also been considered as part of church order. The special characteristic of discipline in the Calvinist tradition inspired the publication of *Books of Discipline,* with the edition by John Knox for Scotland in 1560 being followed in other countries by similar writings.

As early as 1545, in fact, theologians in Wittenberg had thought that church order comprises five elements: the doctrinal part, Scripture and confessions of faith; the administration of the sacraments; the proclamation of the word; church discipline; and religious instruction. In the 20th century a similar concept was formulated by Karl Barth. He identified church order with the life of the community, comprising four theological elements – the confessional community, the baptismal community, the Last Supper community and the community of prayer and worship – which he linked with the *credenda* and *agenda* of the community.

4. The Anglican Church

The English Reformation took place during the reign of King Henry VIII (1491-1547), the leading figure in the events that directly led to a definite rupture with Rome. His marital troubles and his relations with Anne Boleyn led him to ask the pope to dissolve his marriage with Catherine of Aragon. Rome refused, and the king decided to break with the pope and the Church of Rome, convinced that the people of England would support him. Rome was considered the main obstacle to growing nationalism in England. Its nomination of prelates and bishops and the annual taxes to be paid to the pope were seen as direct interference in domestic affairs. One element that had prepared the people for a break with Rome was the ongoing influence of John Wycliffe (1328-1384) and his disciples, the Lollards. Wycliffe's teaching had emphasized the exclusively spiritual nature of the church, and the importance of Scripture as its only law. Though prohibited, translations of the Bible into the vernacular circulated freely, and humanist circles had familiarized the lower clergy and intellectuals with the writings of Martin Luther.

Moreover, the king had as a counsellor the very able and prudent theologian Thomas Cranmer (1489-1556), future archbishop of Canterbury. He helped Henry VIII to undertake a process of liberating the English people and the church in England from the jurisdictional power of Rome. Cranmer made a statement justifying the king's divorce from Catherine of Aragon on theological grounds. Parliament issued a series of decrees to reinforce the king's independent authority and break the resistance of the clergy. A decree in 1531 made Henry VIII the supreme lord and head of the English church. Three years later Parliament ratified the Act of Supremacy by which the king and his successors officially became the supreme head on earth of the Church of England, called *Ecclesia Anglicana*. The king was given full power and authority to repress, reform or correct, restrain and amend all errors, heresies, offences and contempts. Subsequent parliamentary acts sanctioned clerical marriages, suppressed monasteries and replaced unwilling bishops and prelates.

Thus the king had become the exclusive head of the Church of England, with full legislative, executive and judicial power. Theologians explained that the king had received these powers *de iure divino*. The Church of England had become a national state church, an "established church" as it would later be formulated, governed by the king and the parliament.

Cranmer made provisions for the doctrinal, ethical and juridical aspects of the church. A delegation of theologians was sent to Wittenberg to discuss the main features of Luther's teachings. They were told that church legislation, which was to be drafted by bishops and pastors, had no direct relation to salvation, and should not bind people's conscience. It should be inspired by Scripture and guarantee order and peace within the congregations. Following this visit to Germany, a confession of faith of the Anglican Church was formulated in *Ten Articles of Religion* (1539), and approved by Henry VIII. These were replaced in 1562 with the *Thirty-Nine Articles of Religion*, which remain in force to the present day.[22]

It was decided in 1534 that the canons of the Roman Catholic canon law which were not contrary to the new convictions should remain in force in the Church of England. After several attempts, a set of 143 *Constitutions and Canons Ecclesiastical* was approved by the synod of 1603 and by King James I.[23] It begins by emphasizing the supremacy of the king over the Church of England, which is established by law under the king's majesty (Canon 3) and is a true and apostolic church, teaching the doctrines of the apostles. Canons 4 to 12 deal with censures against those who attack articles of religion, rites and ceremonies, and who introduce schism in the church. Canons 13-30 stipulate prescriptions for divine services and the administration of the sacraments. Canon 21 states that communion should be received at least three times a year. The following section (Canons 31-79) is entitled "Ministers, their Ordination, Functions and Charges", and includes a canon on the duties of schoolmasters. Canons 80 to 126 concern objects to be used for worship and the functions of churchwardens. Finally, Canons 127 to 143 regulate the procedures of the courts, sentences and penalties, as well as the conduct of representatives of the clergy in Parliament.

According to Anglican canonist W.J. Hankey, the present canon law of the Church of England comprises Scripture, which "itself is part of Anglican canon law and partly determinative of it", the Apostles' and Nicene Creeds, the *Thirty-Nine Articles of Religion*, the *Book of Common Prayer* and the Ordinal annexed to it, the *Constitutions and Canons*

Ecclesiastical, and those teachings of the ancient fathers and Ecumenical Councils of the church which are in conformity with Scripture. Thus, "Anglican canon law governs moral and spiritual discipline, property and administrative activity of great complexity and diversity".[24] The authority, degree and kind of laws which appear as features of canon law are of a great variety.

The intimate relationship established between church and state by the royal supremacy in the 16th century could not be duplicated in other countries to which Anglicanism spread. Consequently, Anglican canon law received other configurations. For example, the episcopates established in the United States of America in 1784 demanded operating independence from the British Crown. This development was extended by the establishment of Anglican churches in countries that had never been British territory or were not part of the Commonwealth. Parallel to this development, national synods gained the authority to consider themselves as the principle and source of sovereign ecclesiastical legislation. Synods outside England had to take account of the character of their respective legislatures, and canon law had to follow the new constellation. In England itself certain synodal resolutions must be enacted as Acts of Parliament, but "Parliament has exempted itself from considering matters which general synods define as doctrinal. The Royal Licence and Assent also allows general synods to pass canons binding on the clergy in *re ecclesiastica* and enforceably by ecclesiastical courts."[25]

There is a large variety of canon laws in the Anglican Communion, but no central legislative body. However, the English canon lawyer Norman Doc has identified "unifying principles" which, with small variations, characterize all 39 self-governing Anglican churches.[26] A high degree of legal unity can be found in their institutional organization. The independent churches are canonical churches, organized, ordered and governed by canon law. Each claims membership of the one holy, catholic and apostolic church. The highest authority of the independent church is the central assembly, representative of bishops, clergy and laity. The same system exists also in regional, provincial and diocesan churches within the framework of the larger, national church. The general principle is that the church, also in its territorial subdivisions, is synodal. The ancient institution of visitation as a metropolitan and episcopal duty remains in force, and all churches have their own hierarchical courts or tribunal systems.

Another set of unifying principles concerns the laws on the ministry. There is a general rule of threefold ministry: bishops, priests and deacons. Primates generally have limited jurisdiction. Metropolitans have the oversight over the inferior episcopal offices. Diocesan bishops are elected by the clergy, but there are detailed provisions for lay participation in electoral procedures. Diocesan bishops have general oversight over the governing, teaching and liturgical laws and prescriptions. Central commissions generally assist in matters of doctrine, liturgy and discipline. All churches have general agreements and guidelines concerning the sources of doctrine: Scripture, the ancient creeds, the Lord's sacraments, the *Thirty-Nine Articles* and the *Book of Common Prayer*. There are also common rites for the sacraments and common rules for church marriage.

5. A few observations

Church legislation today thus offers a variety of contrasting forms. Two major reasons may be cited to explain how the one Christian faith and the once undivided Christian church have produced such a diversity of church laws. The first is rooted in the very nature of church law. What is its aim and function in the church? More specifically, what is the relationship between church law and the Christian faith? The second is related to the various moments in history in which they emerged. It may even be said that the historical context to a great extent determined the specific nature of the four major Christian confessions dealt with in this chapter.

Notwithstanding the differences, church legislations have several elements in common: (1) All church legislations intend to create and maintain a certain juridical order in the life of the church and to provide guiding principles for the leading, authoritative bodies and their competence. (2) In one or another way, they equip the churches with juridical tools to attain their goal. (3) In one or another way, they are related to the theological and spiritual mission of the church; (4) Generally speaking, the various legislations propose and prescribe norms and guidelines for the members of the church, to fashion their life in conformity with the gospel and the traditional teaching of their church. (5) The majority of the church legislations are directly related to specific confessions of faith.

NOTES

[1] Quoted by Olivier Clément, *Rome autrement: Un Orthodoxe face à la papauté*, Paris, Desclée de Brouwer, 1997, pp.82f.
[2] D. Cummings, ed., *The Rudder (Pedalion) of the Orthodox Church or All the Sacred and Divine Canons*, Chicago, The Orthodox Christian Educational Society, Chicago 1957.
[3] Lewis Patsavos, "The Canonical Tradition of the Orthodox Church", in Fotios K. Litsas, ed., *A Companion to the Greek Orthodox Church*, New York, Archdiocese of North and South America, 1984, p.145.

4 Quotations are from *Code of Canon Law, Latin-English Edition*, translation prepared under the auspices of the Canon Law Society of America, Washington DC, 1983.

5 Text quoted by J.-M. Tillard, *L'Église d'Églises: L'ecclésiologie de communion*, Paris, Cerf, 1987, p.394.

6 *Documentation Catholique*, No. 70, 1973, 670-671.

7 Thomas Aquinas, *Summa Theologiae* I-II, q. 106 ad 1.

8 Eugenio Corecco, "Theologie des Kirchenrechts", in Joseph Listl, Hubert Müller, Heribert Schmitz, eds, *Handbuch des katholischen Kirchenrechts,* Regensburg, Verlag Friedrich Pustet, 1983, p.19.

9 J.-M. Tillard, *op. cit.,* pp.380f.

10 Denzinger, *Enchiridion Symbolorum*, English ed., *The Church Teaches,* Rockford IL, Tan Books and Publishers, 1973, pp.96f.

11 Dogmatic Constitution on the Church: *Lumen Gentium,* para.18, in A. Flannery, ed., *Vatican Council II: The Conciliar and Post-Conciliar Documents,* Northport NY, Castello, 1987.

12 J.-M. Tillard, *L'Église locale: Ecclésiologie de communion et catholicité*, Paris, Cerf, 1995, pp.410-550.

13 Edward Schillebeeckx, *Church: The Human Story of God*, London, SCM Press, 1990, p.219.

14 Martin Luther, *Werke: Kritische Gesamtausgabe, Weimar Ausgabe, Von dem Papstthum zu Rom* (1520), 6, 297, 33-35.

15 *WA* 7, 161-182.

16 *WA* 7, 177, 8-10.

17 *WA*, 180, 11-18.

18 Christoph Strohm, *"Ius divinum* und *ius humanum:* Reformatorische Begründung des Kirchenrechts", in Rau, et al., eds, *Das Recht der Kirche*, Vol. 2, p.150.

19 Calvin, *Institutes,* II.8.2.

20 *Ibid.* IV.11.1-13.

21 Dietrich Dehnen, "Kirchenverfassung und Kirchengesetz", in *Das Recht der Kirche,* Vol. 1, pp.448-73.

22 Cajus Fabricius, ed., *Die Kirche von England: Ihr Gebetbuch, Bekenntnis und Kanonisches Recht,* Berlin und Leipzig, Walter de Gruyter, 1937, pp.374-402.

23 *Ibid.*, pp.465-567.

24 W. J. Hankey, "Canon Law", in Stephen Sykes and John Booty, eds, *The Study of Anglicanism*, London, SPCK, 1988, pp.201ff.

25 *Ibid.,* p.205.

26 Norman Doc, *Canon Law in the Anglican Communion: A Worldwide Perspective*, Oxford, Clarendon Press, 1998.

CHAPTER 3

The Juridical Characteristics:
Historical Contexts

We have suggested that church legislations draw their particular characteristics from the historical origin of the confessional families – that the nuances in the different professions of the one and common Christian faith are determined to a large degree by the specific historical circumstances in which they came into being. We shall look now at how the confessions and consequently the specific legal systems of the churches relate to major events and relevant reactions to the status quo over twenty centuries of church history.

1. The early period

Jewish, Hellenistic or Roman legal systems formed the juridical framework of the emerging Christian communities. In the earliest days the link with Israel was predominant; and for the first Christians, most of whom were Jewish-born, the Torah was the norm for religious and practical life. But soon after the death and resurrection of Jesus a growing awareness arose among the disciples that a new period in the history of Israel had begun. Baptism in the name of the Lord Jesus (Acts 8:16) became the distinctive sign of belonging to the new Jesus community.

The opening of these early communities to non-Jews marked a new phase. At the first council of the apostles, held around A.D. 49 in Jerusalem, it was decided that Jewish law was not to be imposed on non-Jewish Christians (Acts 15). Henceforth it was through baptism alone that people were incorporated in the Christian community. These early Christians saw themselves as pilgrims on earth. Their lives were inspired and guided by the first oral and written testimonies to the words and acts of Jesus, which were outspoken about how Christians should live in obedience to civil authorities and the laws in force.

From the outset the Roman authorities regarded Christianity as a branch of Judaism. Both Jews and Christians enjoyed legal protection. But already by the time of the Neronian persecution in Rome (A.D. 64) a distinction was being made between Jews and Christians. Those who confessed Christ became increasingly liable to punishment. If they rejected the official Roman gods the law considered them as atheists and criminals. Refusal to join in emperor worship led to legal accusations of betrayal and anarchism.

Christianity developed its own characteristics in the second half of the second century, although already in the first century "episcopacy emerged as the dominant form of church order – the rule for each church by a single senior presbyter who took the lead in ordinations and the celebration of the eucharist and who was the focus of unity for all the Christians of a city or a region".[1] Under the guidance of the bishops changes began to take place. Bishops wrote letters to other local communities – Clement of Rome to the Christians of Corinth, Polycarp of Smyrna to the Philippians. Several collections of writings which circulated among these early congregations can be considered as the first juridico-liturgical prescriptions. The *Didache (The Teaching of the Twelve Apostles),* written towards the end of the second century, described ceremonials for baptism and the eucharist and the ministry of bishops, prophets and teachers in an attempt to organize the liturgical and practical details of the Christian way of life and community. The Apostolic Tradition and the Canons of Hippolyte of Rome offered a detailed description of the different ministries in the early third century.

The growing number of local communities called for tighter organization and the elaboration of regulations in different fields. Prescriptions for worship had to be updated. Care for the poor, the sick and widows, the organization of funerals and the upkeep of churches required practical and juridical provisions. Furthermore, the relationships between Christians and the Roman authorities had to be clarified – attitudes towards pagan feasts, Roman public sacrifice services, worship of the emperor and military service, and the treatment of slaves. Roman legislation concerning marriage and conjugal rights and duties had to be adapted to the gospel and already existing Christian customs. Early Christian writers such as Cyprian and Tertullian refer to these concrete matters. Their exegesis of the gospel texts and their exhortations contain many elements which point to future legislation. It was only natural that they made use of existing Roman laws and jurisprudence. Tertullian (around 160-220) speaks of the *lex fidei,* which has to do with the life of faith, and the *lex disciplinae,* which regulates the order and organization of the congregation.

The need was soon felt for cooperation over a wider geographical area, particularly when the appearance of heterodox and false teachings demanded a common position. To facilitate this, lists were circulated of bishops who stayed in contact with one another. Tertullian, in his *De praescriptione haereticorum*, writes: "The unity of the church became apparent in the mutual confirmation of peace, in the guarantee of fraternity and in the amicable signs of hospitality – three features which have no other basis and no other guidance than the one tradition and the one rule of faith."[2]

2. The synodal praxis

Tertullian is one of the first witnesses to the practice of assemblies – called synods or *concilia* – which were attended by bishops, priests, deacons and laity. Letters from Rome, Caesarea and Alexandria to Cyprian, bishop of Carthage (c. 180-250), also refer to annual synods which discussed matters of faith and discipline.[3] In the 3rd century the synodal praxis, which began as an assembly of congregations in one city, became a provincial affair and a diocesan event. When rural parishes came into existence, their pastors and representatives of the laity also were invited to attend these urban synods.

In the course of the 3rd century synods became a permanent element of local and provincial government. Their decisions, expected to be taken unanimously, had to a certain degree the status of law on fundamental questions of doctrine, discipline and church law. Bishops were supposed to follow them. The principle formulated by Cyprian that the bishop is accountable to God alone did not mean that a bishop was entirely free to act according to his own conviction. Synods were also an instrument of communion with neighbouring bishops, invited together with experts and theologians to attend synodal discussions in other cities. In this way, synods increasingly became an awareness-building element in the universal church. Cyprian sees the bishop as the instrument of the common faith and the sacramental order. To be authentically Christian is to be in communion with both the local bishop and the episcopacy as a whole.

Early reports of the agendas and discussions of local and provincial synods indicate that heresies and discipline were features of major importance. The excommunication of heretical and lapsed Christians was a normal measure taken by a bishop. Often such measures were on the agenda of a subsequent synod, which had to see to it that they were communicated to other bishops. Cyprian wrote that a Christian cannot have God for his father and not have the church for his mother. To be outside the communion of the episcopacy and of the assembly of the faithful is "to be outside the ark, drowning in the flood".

The Ecumenical Council of Nicea (325) made the synodal praxis obligatory: Canon 5 prescribed that a provincial synod should be celebrated in the whole church every two years. Already with the Edict of Milan (313) synodal praxis had received a new dimension as a consequence of the alliance between church and state. By granting full freedom to Christianity, this declaration of the Emperor Constantine (c. 270-337) signified a revolution in the relationship between Christianity and the state, the Roman empire. The new situation was not merely one of tolerance; legally, Christianity now stood on equal footing with all other recognized religions of the empire. A further edict issued in 380 by the emperors Gratian, Valentinian II and Theodosius I established Christianity as the official state religion of the empire.

Constantine was not slow to draw the consequences of the Edict of Milan; and historians refer to a gathering in Rome in 313 as the first imperial synod. It was convened by the emperor, who chaired the discussions. According to Eusebius of Caesarea (c. 260-340), Constantine organized several local and provincial synods in this way. He saw his role as mediating in conflicts and promoting peace. In doctrinal discussions he shared the decisions taken by bishops.

Twelve years after the Edict of Milan all elements were at hand to celebrate the first imperial and universal synod. Constantine took the initiative of inviting the bishops to Nicea in 325. He informed them about the exact opening time and proposed agenda, and also took charge of all expenses. The synodal decisions followed the already existing distinction between doctrinal issues and those dealing with juridical and disciplinary matters. Wherever necessary the emperor declared synodal decisions to be imperial laws.

The active and often decisive role played by Constantine in the universal synod was not alien to law and tradition in the Roman Empire. As *Pontifex Maximus,* the emperor had the authority to watch over the public aspect of religion. In practice this meant that from Constantine's days on the emperor, together with the episcopacy, took responsibility for church government and the maintenance of church laws and liturgical prescriptions. By means of Constantine's role as *Pontifex Maximus* the traditional imperial system continued. This became even more relevant when Christianity became the official religion of the empire in 380 and was integrated in the imperial state. The consequences of this new status for Christianity were important. Decisions made about doctrine, discipline and other ecclesiastical matters, especially when ratified by the emperor or other civil authorities, became state laws. This was the beginning of the one and only legal order that regulated both church and civil life. As a uniform legal system this survived into the Middle Ages.

The new constellation meant an advantage for the Christian church. The imperial synods turned it into a body that guaranteed doctrinal unity as well as the unity of the church, since canons and decisions taken by the imperial synods were received and applied universally. In doctrinal matters, the imperial synods guaranteed orthodoxy against heresies. Transgressions were punished by church and state measures, and judged in courts.

3. Rome and the primacy of the Roman pontiff

The Christian church established in Rome around the year 40 differed from those in such cities as Antioch and Carthage.[4] While Christianity in Rome, as elsewhere, grew out of the synagogue, no co-ordinating centre existed for the 40 or so independent synagogues in Rome, which were all related to their places of origin in Syria, Greece and Asia Minor. In the same way, the first Christian congregations in Rome were independent from one another. Unlike other city churches, the congregations in the capital, given their ethnic and cultural diversity, were reluctant to adopt a system of co-ordination by a bishop. The Christian community there was thus a loose and often divided federation of different congregations.

Not until the middle of the 3rd century were the words of Jesus recorded in Matthew 16:16-18 – "You are Peter and upon this rock I will build my church" – applied to the bishop of Rome, where Peter was buried. And then, as Eamon Duffy observes, "the claims which the bishop of Rome of the time tried to base on that quotation were indignantly rejected by the churches of Africa to whom he was addressing himself".[5] In fact, this passage in Matthew and related texts in Luke (9:22-23) and John (21:15-17) were interpreted in different ways almost from the outset. Alongside the understanding that "this rock" refers to Peter were affirmations that it is Jesus Christ himself or the faith in Christ as confessed by Peter on which the church is built.

Historians today agree that the emergence of the bishop of Rome and his authority were not the direct result of a concrete and immediate act of Jesus during his life on earth, but rather of a long and uncertain historical process. Certainly in the mid-3rd-century dispute referred to above, the authority of the bishop of Rome over and above the other bishops was by no means a matter of fact. On that occasion, Bishop Stephen, referred to as the bishop of Rome, and Bishop Cyprian of Carthage differed sharply over the question of baptism. Stephen asserted that all should observe the tradition of Peter and Paul, namely that those who were baptized by heretical clergy should be re-admitted as penitents by the laying-on of hands. Cyprian's vehement dissent was supported by the Greek East. Cyprian thought it was absurd to suppose that, where there is no true eucharist because of a schism or heresy, there can be a valid baptism. At this point the bishop of Rome invoked for the first time the text of Matthew to justify his jurisdictional authority.[6]

The original situation of the Christian community in Rome as we have described it made it easy prey to schismatic and heretical "prophets". The threat of heresy together with the traditionally Roman demand for order and unity led to the establishment of the Roman episcopate, with as its centre the two graves of Peter and Paul. The head of the Roman episcopate thus came to be considered as the successor of the Apostle Peter and received the title "pope".

The growing authority which led to the primacy of the bishop of Rome is again the product of an historical evolution. At the third Ecumenical Council in Ephesus (431) the papal legate exhorted the bishops to carry out the decisions of Pope Celestine (422-432) regarding Nestorius in these words:

> No one doubts, in fact it is obvious, that the holy and most blessed Peter, head and prince of the apostles, the pillar of faith, and the foundation of the Catholic church, received the keys of the kingdom from our Lord Jesus Christ... Nor does anyone doubt that the power of forgiving and retaining sins was also given to the same Peter who, in his successors, lives and exercises judgment even to this time and forever.[7]

From the pontificate of Pope Gelasius (492-496) to that of Pope Hormisdas (514-523), awareness of the unique authority of the bishop of Rome continued to evolve. Gelasius affirmed his authority over against Emperor Anastasius I of Constantinople, insisting in a letter to him that the emperor's power is subordinated to the authority of the bishop of Rome, since "the See of St Peter cannot be judged by anyone". Gelasius also took responsibility for filing council documents and papal decretals in one single legal corpus, with the aim of unifying and coordinating church legislation under the pope's authority and of making it universally binding.

Under Pope Hormisdad, the Emperor Justinian ordered the bishops of the East to sign a profession of faith referring to the universally binding nature of the text of Matthew 16:16-18.

> The truth has been proved by the course of history, for in the Apostolic See religion has always been kept unsuspected. From this hope and faith we by no means desire to be separated... Following the Apostolic See in all things we endorse and approve all the letters which Pope Leo wrote concerning the Christian religion. And so I hope we may deserve to be associated with you in the one communion which the Apostolic See proclaims, in which the whole, true and perfect security of the Christian religion resides. I promise that from now on those who are separated from the communion of the Catholic Church, that is, who are not in agreement with the Apostolic See, will not have their names read during the sacred mysteries.[8]

Several centuries later, pope Leo IX (1049-1054) wrote to Patriarch Michael Cerularius of Constantinople that

> the holy church has been built upon a rock, that is, upon Christ, and upon Peter..., in a way that it never was to be conquered... by heretical opinions... Is it not by the See of the prince of the apostles, namely, by this Roman church, both by this same Peter and by his successors, that all the inventions of heretics stand condemned, exposed and overcome? Are not the hearts of the brethren strengthened in the faith of Peter which has not failed thus far and will not fail till the end of time?[9]

A document that was decisive for theologians and canon lawyers seeking to establish the supremacy of the bishop of Rome in both ecclesiastical and temporal affairs is the so-called *Donatio Constantiniana* or "Donation of Constantine".[10] While its text claims that it was written personally by the Emperor Constantine, it has been recognized since the Renaissance to be a forgery by an unknown author of Frankish origin, written between 750 and 800. Leo IX was the first pope to use the text to undergird his authority, in 1054. The *Donatio* is written in the form of a letter from the Emperor Constantine to "the most holy and blessed father Sylvester, bishop of the city of Rome and pope, and to all his successors, the pontiffs, who shall occupy the See of the blessed Peter until the end of time". After a confession of faith and an account of the emperor's recovery from leprosy, the document affirms that Constantine wants to give Sylvester and his successors "greater governmental power" and "to exalt the most holy See of blessed Peter in glory above our own empire and earthly throne, ascribing to it glorious majesty and strength and imperial honour". Therefore, the text continues:

> We command and decree that the Bishop of Rome should have primacy over the four principal Sees of Antioch, Alexandria, Constantinople and Jerusalem, and that the pontiff of Rome shall rank as the highest and chief among all the priests of the whole world and by his decision all things are to be arranged concerning the worship of God or the security of the faith of Christians... We give to the most holy pontiff, our Father Sylvester, the universal pope, not only the Lateran Palace, but also the city of Rome and all the provinces, districts and cities of Italy and the western regions, relinquishing them to the authority of himself and his successors as laid down by this our divine, holy and lawfully framed decree; and we grant it on a permanent legal basis to the holy Roman church.

The *Donatio Constantiniana* served as an example for the *Dictatus* of Pope Gregory VII (1073-1085), appearing in his official register under the title "What is the Power of the Roman Pontiff?"[11] These 27 *dicta* set out a summary of the principles that should inspire pontifical policy-making, holding up the ideal of a Christian society under the strong leadership of the bishop of Rome. Among other things, the document states

> that the Roman church was founded by God alone; that the Roman pontiff alone can rightly be called universal; that he alone can depose or re-instate bishops; that he alone may use and dispose of imperial insignia; that it may be permitted him to depose emperors; that he himself may be judged by none; that he may absolve subjects from their fealty to wicked men.

Pope Gregory set in motion an important reform movement. He strongly re-affirmed the primacy of the bishop of Rome over the universal church. The primatial authority of the Roman pontiff had now become a reality. At the same time, he strenuously affirmed the supremacy of the papacy over temporal authorities and publicly forbade any lay investiture in ecclesiastical offices.

The supremacy of the Roman pontiff as conceived by Pope Gregory VII entered into the legal system of the Roman Catholic Church by way of the *Decretum Gratiani,* composed around 1140 by the Italian monk Gratian.[12] This decree, appearing in the early manuscripts under the title *Concordia discordantium canonum,* aims to provide a rigorous *summa* of the canonical tradition. As such, it constitutes the first juridical corpus of the church. Gratian attempts to demonstrate that conflicts among differing opinions and doctrines can be attributed to different interpretations of terms and as such are more apparent than real. He introduces a new element into canon law, namely theology, considering the texts of the Hebrew Bible and the New Testament as authoritative sources of Christian church law. For Gratian the sacred texts constitute *ius naturale* and *ius divinum positivum.*

According to the *Decretum,* the bishop of Rome is the undisputed source, guardian and master of canon law, the head and absolute primate of the church in virtue of God's law, *de iure divino.* Gratian's decree thus introduced a legal system of divine, natural and ecclesiastical laws in which God, the supreme legislator, has delegated power, including legislative power, to the Roman pontiff, the successor of the prince of the apostles, St Peter.

Hence, from the moment Christianity was installed as the official religion of the Roman empire – and, even more so, from the moment the church and its supreme head took the place of the declining empire – canon law became the dominant factor guiding both church and society. In fact, it became the uniting link and ideological foundation of the entire mediaeval order, the guarantee for the institutional and hierarchical physiognomy of the Roman Catholic Church. This physiognomy is upheld by the Church of Rome to the present day and constitutes the heart of canon law.

The supremacy of the Roman pontiff over temporal affairs was also formulated in canon law. While the emperors too received their authority from God, their authority was believed to come through the intermediary role of the church. Often they tried to break the pope's supremacy by attacking his authority and supreme power in temporal affairs. However, the popes, understanding themselves as vicars of Christ, increasingly defended their right to interfere in the temporal order, more than once turning secular authorities into humble dependents. Over the centuries this supremacy of the Roman pontiff has been consistently safeguarded, notably by Pope Innocent III (1198-1216), by Pope Boniface VIII (1294-1303) in his Bull *Unam Sanctam*,[13] and by the *Syllabus Errorum*, issued by Pope Pius IX in 1864.[14]

4. The division between East and West

The life of the church in the East during the early Byzantine period was dominated by the seven general councils. In the words of Kallistos Ware, these assemblies fulfilled the double function of clarifying and articulating the visible organization of the church and defining once and for all its teaching on the fundamental Christian doctrines of the Trinity and the Incarnation. Since these are "mysteries" which lie beyond human understanding and language, the doctrinal definitions produced by the seven Ecumenical Councils – Nicea I (325) to Nicea II (787) – did not explain the Trinity and the Incarnation, but sought to exclude false ways of thinking and speaking about them: "to prevent people from deviating into error and heresy, they drew a fence around the mystery".[15]

Though within the tradition of synodal praxis, the seven Ecumenical Councils had a universal character, and bishops from the entire world attended them, well aware that they acted as a college, collegially. Orthodox theologian Olivier Clément speaks of a "creative tension" between the praxis of the Ecumenical Councils and the claims of the Roman pontiff. The Church of Rome was considered the most venerable among all the churches and the bishop of Rome was respected especially because he watched over the unity of the faith; but, says Clément,

> the real grandeur of the era of the Ecumenical Councils is to be found precisely in the fact that no one could decide, neither the pope, nor the council, nor the emperor, nor popular sensibility. Everyone claimed to have the last word, and so no one had it, except for sure, the Holy Spirit.[16]

However, the historical process that eventually led to the recognition of the primacy of the Roman pontiff in the Western church was already evident from the 5th century onwards. The source of the definitive break between the Eastern and Western churches was not exclusively theological: cultural, political and linguistic differences were inextricably tangled up with theological issues.

The transfer of the imperial residence from Rome to Constantinople in 330 was the first major source of mistrust, rivalry and even jealousy between West and East; and when the Ecumenical Council of Chalcedon in the mid-5th century made Constantinople the second most important patriarchate after Rome, the Roman delegation protested. Contacts between the two parts of the undivided church were weakened by the barbarian invasions in the West. The statement of Pope Pelagius (495) that the power of the emperor in Constantinople was subordinate to the authority of the bishop of Rome caused much rancour in both imperial and church circles in the East. Moreover, as time passed, the homogeneity and unity of the Mediterranean world was rapidly vanishing. The rise of Islam, its conquest of most of the Mediterranean regions and the arrival of the Slavs in the Balkans further intensified mutual alienation between East and West. Communication between the two parts became increasingly difficult because of language problems; and each side developed its own culture.

Illustrative of the widening gap were Pope Gregory III's appeal to Charles Martel to help him against the Lombards and the pope's coronation of Charlemagne in 800, reviving a Western Roman empire.

> In the eyes of Constantinople, the West acted as if the Roman empire, with its legitimate emperor in Constantinople, had ceased to exist. The Byzantine empire's claims to world sovereignty were being ignored. Charlemagne's new empire was usurping the legitimate role of the Roman empire in Constantinople. Such a declaration of independence and emancipation from Byzantium seemed to threaten the unity of Christendom and, indirectly, the shared faith of the one church.[17]

Other causes of the division were theological and ecclesiological. One such area of difference was the theology of the Holy Spirit, illustrated in the *filioque* controversy. The original creed from the Ecumenical Councils of Nicea and Constantinople stated that the Holy Spirit, the Lord and Giver of life, "proceeds from the Father". The addition by the Western church of the words "and from the Son" *(filioque)* was considered unacceptable and heretical in the East. Moreover, the interpretation was unilateral: the Eastern church should at least have been consulted. The papal bull of excommunication placed on the altar of the Church of Holy Wisdom in Constantinople in 1054 turned this theological dispute into a highly political event. The Gregorian Reform of the 11th century completed the division. Church and civil authorities in the East saw in the *Dictatus* of Pope Gregory VII, proclaiming the unlimited authority and universal jurisdiction over the entire church of the Roman pontiff, an unacceptable violation of the essentially collegial, conciliar and democratic nature of the church. The Orthodox thus impute the schism to the Roman Church and consider their own church as the authentic one which has preserved the faith as given by the gospel and Tradition:

> There is, according to the dogmatic tradition of the Orthodox church, a living continuity between the apostolic community of the early church and the community that succeeds to it. The same faith, teachings, doctrine and Christian life continue to be present and perpetuate themselves throughout the history of the church. In this sense, the church continues to be apostolic, that is, in living continuity with the early Christian apostolic community. Tradition, as the life of the church, is seen in terms of this living community with our Christian origins.[18]

5. Movements of reform and dissent

The concentration of religious power in the person of the bishop of Rome and his claim to absolute primacy had forced the Eastern Christians to liberate themselves from the spiritual yoke of Rome. But this was to be only the beginning of a far-reaching process that would change the religious map of Europe. Historical events during the 14th century worsened the situation. Both the empire and the papacy were in decline. The captivity of the bishop of Rome in Avignon (1305-1378), followed by the Great Schism of popes and obediences (1378-1429), undermined the credibility of the papacy, giving birth to new religious élan and enthusiasm in favour of fundamental reform. The desire to reform and change the church *in capite et membris* became a slogan that permeated all levels of the Christian world:

> It was a time of transition and, as such, characterized by anxiety as well as achievement. This was evident in the Western conception of God at this time... The people in Europe were more concerned about their faith than ever before. They were dissatisfied with the mediaeval forms of religion that no longer answered their needs... Indeed, Europe seemed obsessed by God.[19]

However, in many European countries Rome and the church turned a deaf ear to the cries for change. Instead of discerning the signs of the times, they responded with the procedure of "inquiries" that "suspended the normal rights of defendants, which in mediaeval law were very extensive".[20] The Inquisition became a feared instrument to crush dissent.

The first reaction to this state of affairs came from the Brethren of Common Life and the spiritual movement they inspired. They represented a general quest for holiness which arose in the Hanseatic cities of the Low Countries, Germany and Switzerland. The Brethren promoted mysticism as a natural consequence of consistent ascetic and spiritual life. This was a reaction against the rational scholastic theology officially endorsed by Rome, which taught that God can be known only as he reveals himself in the Bible as rightly and exclusively interpreted by the church, and that the sacraments of the church guarantee the salvation of the faithful. The Brethren insisted that God can also be known through mystical experience. In mysticism all creation depends on God's love, and in God's love all creatures are interdependent, since through the divine spark, alive in a person's innermost self, all creatures become manifestations of the love of God. Mysticism thus implies a holistic worldview. Church authorities distrusted this, not only because it could lead to pantheism but also because knowledge about God acquired through God's indwelling in the human person could neither be verified nor controlled. Even less did it leave to the church its role as sacrament of salvation. Therefore, one of the greatest exponents of mysticism, Meister Eckhardt (1270-1327), was accused of heresy by church authorities and a number of his writings were condemned for alleged pantheism.

Another mystic was Catherine of Siena (1347-1380), a member of the vast Beguine movement which had arisen in the early 12th century. Some Beguines lived on their own, as did Mechteld of Magdeburg (1210-1283) and Julian of Norwich (1342-1417); others formed semi-monastic groupings, as did Hildegard von Bingen (1098-1197), in the Netherlands, Belgium, Germany, France and England. They attached great importance to reading and meditating on the Scriptures. Their ideal was to live a life of poverty after the example of Jesus. Many were very critical of the wealth and the temporal ambitions of church authorities; and since they did not enjoy any authoritative protection, many Beguines were accused of witchcraft and condemned by the Inquisition.

Among the first lay protagonists of the popular poverty movement which began around 1175 were the followers of a merchant of Lyons, in France, named Valdes, or Peter Valdo. For these "Poor of Lyons" poverty was directly linked with faithfulness to the primary source of the church, the Scripture, and the itinerant proclamation of a life in conformity with the gospel. Thus they asked for official permission to preach. However, the Third Lateran Council reaffirmed the provision formulated in the Decree of Gratian, which allowed a lay person to preach only at the explicit invitation of a clergyman. But by and large the followers of Peter Valdo, whose numbers grew rapidly, ignored this measure; their movement soon spread to Italy, Spain, Austria, Germany and Bohemia. While they were excommunicated by the Fourth Lateran Council (1215) and condemned as heretics, the Waldensians, as they came to be called, considered themselves as dissenters, convinced that they were continuing the life of the early Christians.

One of the legends the Waldensians transmitted from generation to generation narrated the history of the *Donatio Constantiniana* in terms of Constantine's gift to Pope Sylvester as marking a real break with the authentic church initiated by Jesus Christ. By accepting dominion over Italy and the entire West, the pope had made a fatal mistake. From that moment on, greed, wealth and power in the church had replaced humble, spiritual Christian life in conformity with the gospel. The apostolic witness, the authentic tradition of the Christian faith, the faith of the early church, could not continue to exist in a church that had fundamentally betrayed its calling. But the true church of Christ was still alive, although hidden and clandestine: the church of a friend of Pope Sylvester, as the legend had it, who warned the pope of the great danger, having heard a voice from heaven announcing the disaster.

This Waldensian legend was not an isolated story. Beginning in the 12th century, explicit criticism of the *Donatio Constantiniana* was often voiced. The 14th-century English poet William Langland wrote:

> When Constantine endowed the church so generously, and gave it lands and vassals, estates and incomes, an angel was heard to cry in the air over the city of Rome, saying: "This day the wealth of the church is poisoned, and those who have Peter's power have drunk venom."[21]

This story of the angel was widespread in the Middle Ages.

Recent studies link the Waldensians with what scholars have come to call the First Reformation, which also embraced such movements and groups as the Czechoslovak Hussite Church, the Unity of Brethren and the renewed Moravian Church, the Czech Brethren and several Hussite-based churches. All these movements focused on the synoptic gospels, especially on the Sermon on the Mount as a rule of life. The First Reformation was marked by a strong eschatological emphasis on the coming reign of Christ, the direct action of the Holy Spirit not mediated by the church and the ethical demands of the gospel in the life of individuals and the congregation. The number of dissenting groups and individuals to whom the term "First Reformation" can be applied increased steadily between the 13th and 15th centuries. Most of these rejected the Church of Rome primarily because of its alliance with states and civil authorities. The Constantinian order was considered as the major obstacle to a truly Christian life and a truly Christian society.

In summary, the characteristics of the First Reformation may be identified as:

1. A preference for the gospels, especially for the Sermon on the Mount, where believers directly find Christ's model of life as well as his teaching. Both clearly reveal God's will, which believers are to follow in every respect.
2. The important role of the Old Testament. The old law gives valid ethical instruction when it is understood more radically on the basis of the New Law, in the sense of the antitheses of the Sermon on the Mount.
3. The New Law as the binding norm not only for individual life, but also for forming social structures.
4. The Christian as a follower of the suffering Christ. The Christ of the gospels provides his disciples with a script for life.[22]

A major protagonist of the First Reformation was the Czech Jan Huss (1369-1415). He taught that the church is constituted by the chosen ones. According to Huss, the head of the church is not the bishop of Rome but Christ; and the model for the life of the church should be the poverty of Christ. Huss severely criticized the wealth of the clergy and condemned the exercise of physical force by order of the pope or other church authorities. Moreover, he argued that payments could not produce forgiveness in God's sight and that indulgences had value for the elect alone. Huss was condemned and Prague was placed under papal interdict. He went into exile and wrote a treatise *On the Church*. Huss did not reject the church in its totality, and it was only after his condemnation that he called the pope the Antichrist. At the Council of Constance he was burned as a heretic.

In many ways Huss was a disciple of the Oxford professor John Wycliffe (1328-1384). Wycliffe taught that both civil and ecclesiastical authority belong to God, and that those in authority are nothing more than stewards. Because God gave the lordship over temporal affairs to civil authorities, temporal affairs in the hands of unworthy clergy should be taken away from them by civil authorities. When Pope Gregory X ordered him to examine these teachings, Wycliffe focused on reform issues. He stated that Scripture constitutes the only law of the church, which is the body of the elect, those who follow Christ as the early Christians did. Wycliffe did not reject the papacy, but taught that the bishop of Rome should be, in theory and practice, one of the elect, an example of the chosen ones in restoring the life of the early church. A pope who strives after worldly power and exacts taxes is non-elect and hence against Christ.

Besides seeing to the translation of the Latin Vulgate Bible into English, Wycliffe sent out "poor priests", living in apostolic poverty, to proclaim the gospel two by two. In 1382 a synod in London condemned

24 theses taught by Wycliffe. After his death his disciples, the Lollards, continued to spread his teachings.

Wycliffe was probably the first person directly to attack the mediaeval Roman concept of law, but he was soon followed by others; and in this way the road was prepared for the Reformers. The rector of the University of Paris, Marsilius of Padua (1275-1342) advanced the thesis that all power belongs to the people. Hence, power in the church belongs to the whole body of believers, who appoint the rulers of the state and the church. They also decide in a general council on matters of Christian faith and morals; and its decisions have supreme authority in church affairs. In the church the New Testament constitutes the only definitive authority. According to the Bible, bishops and priests are equal, but it is appropriate to appoint some of the clergy as superintendents, with a limited administrative function. Nor does the pope have jurisdiction over other priests or bishops. Peter had no higher rank than the other apostles; moreover, there is no evidence in the Bible that Peter was ever in Rome. The New Testament does not support the idea that members of the clergy may possess earthly lordship or estates.

William of Ockham (1300-1349), a contemporary of Marsilius, studied in Oxford and became a professor at the University of Paris. One of his teachings was that Jesus Christ and the apostles lived in complete poverty. Basing the Christian faith on the authority of Scriptures, both the Hebrew Bible and the New Testament, Ockham attacked theology that overemphasized its rational character to the detriment of another aspect of the Tradition of the church, namely the need for a personal experience of God through the action of the Holy Spirit.

The humanist Erasmus of Rotterdam (1469-1536) considered canon law "a tyrannically pretentious document, full of unjust and loveless prescriptions, exploitation and immorality".[23] Applying to canon law the *aequitas naturalis* of Roman law, Erasmus rejected several parts of it. Like other humanists he was convinced that the Bible contains all aspects of the law of Christ, including equality, and that the historical development of canon law, which at the outset offered guidelines for Christian morality, had gone the wrong direction, losing its orientation to the Christian commandment of love, which was the foundation of Erasmus' Christian philosophy. Since canon law has no absolute character, it should be changed in order to keep pace with the course of history.

6. The Reformation and its aftermath

The Reformation was a period of great fear among both its followers and those who remained faithful to Rome. There were violent repudiations of the past, bitter condemnations and anathemas, a terror of heresy and doctrinal deviations, an over-awareness of sin. People were obsessed by hell. Thousands died as martyrs for fundamentally similar religious convictions. By the end of the 16th century religion had been seriously discredited by the killing of Protestants by Catholics and Catholics by Protestants.[24]

With the appearance of Lutheran and Reformed churches, Rome lost its centuries'-old monopoly. Large numbers of Christians no longer accepted its doctrine or its form of church government. In the temporal realm it had been deprived in many places of the protection of the state-church alliance. The Council of Trent (1545-1563) aimed to restore Rome's religious power and re-affirm its teaching. It laid the dogmatic and canonical foundations for an internal reform of the church that anchored it even more firmly in the primacy of the pope.

Tridentine canon law did not abolish the previous canon law, but supplemented it with doctrinal and disciplinary decisions. The Council defined the teaching of the Roman Catholic Church over and against the "heretical" doctrines of the Reformers, adopting numerous canons – about justification, the sacraments, priestly orders, the mass, the Mother of God and the saints, Tradition and Scripture, purgatory and indulgences – of the form: "If anyone says...," followed by the view of the Reformers, followed by, "Let him be anathema."

Since canon law was considered the main instrument of defence against the Protestant "enemies", both church legislation as such and its interpretation and jurisprudence were narrowed. Commentaries on the canons offered no more than a literal exegesis of the text, and little attention was paid to their theological roots. Reason as the ideological foundation of law – as taught by Aristotle and Aquinas – was replaced by the will of the legislator, the Roman pontiff. The situation is summarized in the decree *Benedictus Deus*, issued by Pope Pius IV in 1564:

> To avoid any perversion and confusion, which could arise if it were permitted to anyone who so wished to publish his own comments and interpretations on the decrees of the Council of Trent, with apostolic authority we order that... no one must publish, in any way whatsoever, without authorization, commentaries, glossaries, annotations, scholia or interpretations of any kind concerning the Council's decrees; or to state anything in anybody's name about them, not even with the aim of giving greater strength to them, or promoting their implementation.[25]

Following the trend of the replacement of the old political system of empire by a constellation of independent states and regions, the churches of the Reformation had become territorial churches. The response of Rome was to proclaim the Roman Catholic Church a "perfect society". This is a technical term for a society that has its own legal system and all the juridical means necessary to reach its own ends without depending on any other society. As a consequence, says Ladislas Örsy, "elements of secular organization and jurisprudence were increasingly imported into the community of believers, whether on a superficial level, as in some titles and offices, or in more substantial matters, such as the increasing centralization in the government of the church".[26]

In 1885, Pope Leo XIII's encyclical letter *Immortale Dei* gave a theological and legal foundation to the concept of the church as a perfect society. This society was characterized as *Ius Publicum Ecclesiasticum*. The Church of Rome had to be considered as sovereign and independent from all other entities whatsoever in order to establish its own laws and to maintain these with sanctions against transgressions. The theory of the church as a perfect society dominates the Code of Canon Law issued in 1917. Alongside, above and independently from the legal systems of secular states, the Church of Rome forms a universal, sovereign, autonomous religious legal order, based on the universal, immediate legal power of the Roman pontiff over the entire church.[27]

NOTES

[1] Eamon Duffy, "The Popes: Theory and Fact", *The Tablet*, 4 July 1998, p.871.
[2] Quoted by Adolf Martin Ritter, "Reich und Konzil", in Rau, et al., eds, *Das Recht der Kirche*, Vol. 2. p.41.
[3] Cf. Jean-Marie Tillard, *L'Eglise locale*, pp.333-45.
[4] Henry Chadwick, "The Early Christian Community", in J. McManners, ed., *The Oxford Illustrated History of Christianity*, Oxford, Oxford U.P., 1992, p.37.
[5] Eamon Duffy, *loc.cit.*, p.871.
[6] Chadwick, *loc.cit.*, p.36.
[7] Denzinger, *Enchiridion Symbolorum;* English edition, *The Church Teaches*, p.69.
[8] *Ibid.*, pp.70f.
[9] *Ibid.*, p.71.
[10] Marc Reuver, *Requiem for Constantine*, Kok, Kampen, 1996, pp.55f.
[11] *Ibid.*, p.63.
[12] Cf. Jean Gaudemet, *Eglise et Cité: Histoire du droit canonique*, Paris, Cerf-Montchrestien, 1994.
[13] Denzinger, pp.73-75.
[14] Marc Reuver, *op. cit.*, pp.176-77.
[15] Timothy Ware, *The Orthodox Church*, London, Penguin, 2d ed., 1993, p.20.
[16] Olivier Clément, *Rome autrement*, p.63.
[17] Aristeides Papadakis, "History of the Orthodox Church", in Litsas, ed., *A Companion to the Greek Orthodox Church*, pp.18f.
[18] Maximos Aghiorgoussis, "The Dogmatic Tradition of the Orthodox Church", in *ibid.*, p.149.
[19] Karen Armstrong, *A History of God*, London, Mandarin, 1993, p.296.
[20] Colin Morris, "Christian Civilization", in *The Oxford Illustrated History of Christianity*, p.215; see also Jacob Sprenger Heinrich Institoris, *Der Hexenhammer: Malleus maleficarum*, ed. J.W.R. Schmidt, Munich, Deutscher Taschenbuch Verlag, 1993.
[21] William Langland, *Piers the Ploughman*, Part 2, Book 15, Tr. J.F. Goodridge, Harmondsworth, UK, Penguin, 1966, p.194; cf. also Barbara Tuchman, *A Distant Mirror: The Calamitous 14th Century*, London, MacMillan, 1994, p.6.
[22] Cf. Milan Opocensky, ed., *Towards a Renewed Dialogue: The First and Second Reformations*, Geneva, World Alliance of Reformed Churches, 1996, p.35.

23 W. Maurer, *Erasmus und das kanonisches Recht*, quoted by Christoph Strohm, *"Ius divinum* und . *ius humanum"*, in *Das Recht der Kirche,* Vol. II, p.121.
24 Karen Armstrong, *op. cit.* p.29.
25 Denzinger, no. 1849.
26 Ladislas Örsy, *Theology and Canon Law,* pp.25f.
27 *Codex Iuris Canonici*, auctoritate Benedicti Papae XV promulgatus, Typis Polyglottis Vaticanis, 1918.

CHAPTER 4

Confessions of Faith and Church Legislations

While Scripture constitutes the primary source and unique criterion for church legislation, confessions of faith and creeds are also an important source of church laws. Theologically derived directly from the Bible, they generally offer contextual interpretations of the sacred texts. Taken together, Scripture, confessions of faith, church laws, constitutions and fundamental Christian rights may be seen as making up a composite whole called *church order*.

1. Confessions of faith

The confessions of faith fall into two distinct categories, the first dating back to early Christianity, the second originating in the historical period of the Reformation and Counter-Reformation.

The *Apostles' Creed* is certainly one of the oldest confessions of faith. This title appears for the first time in a document issued by the Synod of Milan (390), and for many centuries no one doubted that it had been the apostles who put together this summary of the faith taught and lived by the Lord. Later, however, its authority was questioned by the Council of Florence (1438-1445).

The *Nicene Creed* (325) was promulgated at the first Council of Nicea. According to tradition it was based on the baptismal creed of Caesarea. Although not directly intended to be a baptismal creed, it greatly influenced the revision of the confessions of faith then in use.

While the origins of the *Nicene-Constantinopolitan Creed* are not known, it is certain that after the Councils of Ephesus (431) and Chalcedon (451) it made its way into the liturgy of the Eastern Church, where it soon became the baptismal creed. It was introduced into the Western liturgy towards the end of the 8th century; and studies by the Commission on Faith and Order and the Joint Working Group between the Roman Catholic Church and the WCC have concluded that it is the only creed shared by churches of Eastern and Western traditions.

Günther Gassmann has written that "one of the undisputed presuppositions of all ecumenical endeavours towards manifesting the unity of the church was and is that there must be unity in faith".[1] The fifth assembly of the World Council of Churches (Nairobi 1975) placed the issue of the common confession of the apostolic faith squarely on the ecumenical agenda. "We ask the churches to undertake a common effort to receive, reappropriate and confess together, as contemporary occasion requires, the Christian truth and faith, delivered through the apostles and handed down through the centuries."[2] During the 1980s the WCC Faith and Order Commission organized intensive studies *Towards the Common Expression of the Apostolic Faith Today;*[3] and the seventh assembly of the WCC (Canberra 1991) called all churches "to move towards the recognition of the apostolic faith as expressed through the Nicene-Constantinopolitan Creed in the life and witness of one another".[4]

Two other creeds may be mentioned in this survey. There exist both long and short versions of the *Creed of Epiphanius,* composed in response to numerous requests for a clear and exact explanation of Catholic doctrine in the context of controversies about the Trinity, and specifically about the Holy Spirit. The longer version was meant to refute doctrinal errors, while the shorter formulation was used to instruct catechumens before admission to baptism.

The exact date of *the Athanasian Creed* is not certain, but it was probably composed in the 5th or 6th century, and it is doubtful that Athanasius (c. 293-373) is the author. In the 8th century this creed, known also as *Quicumque vult*, after the first words of its Latin text, was introduced into the liturgical books of the West. While its widespread and persistent use has given it great authority, and it is still used in the Roman Catholic and Anglican churches, it has generally given way to the Nicene-Constantinopolitan Creed.

The second series of confessions of faith grew out of the diffusion of the ideas of the Reformation. German princes asked Luther to write down his ideas about the major issues of the Christian faith; similar requests were addressed to his disciple Melanchthon and to John Calvin. These first writings were followed by a certain number of confessions and catechisms, issued by the first and second generation of Reformers and by local, provincial or national synods. The 17th century saw the appearance of the Canons of the Synod of Dordrecht (1619) and the Westminster Confession of Faith (1647), which are numbered among the original confessions of the Reformation. In 1564 Pope Pius VI introduced the Creed of the Council of Trent, which summarizes the Tridentine doctrines against the supposed errors taught by the Reformers.

The key difference between the confessions of faith of the early church and those which originated in the time of the Reformation is that the former were written in and for an undivided church. They were contextual in that they formulated fundamental Christian teaching over against heresies or doctrinal disputes and controversies. The confessions of faith of the 16th and 17th centuries were written primarily to identify the differences between Reformation and Roman Catholic doctrines. While the Reformation confessions underline the common characteristics of the new Reformation doctrines, they also accentuate the specificity of the particular Reformed family from which they emerge. Thus the various confessions of faith mark the diverging identities of Lutheranism, Calvinism and Anglicanism. As a consequence, church legislations reflect the same differences.

This development gave birth to a new theological science, called *Konfessionskunde* or symbolics. Its object is to arrive at a typology of the different confessions of faith and the different confessional families and churches constituted on the basis of them.[5] As analytical studies of the similarities and differences among Lutheran, Calvinist and Anglican confessions have continued, earlier polemics have slowly lost their sharp edges, and there has been a growing tendency to emphasize the elements which confessional families and churches have in common.

But even the most irenic scholar cannot ignore the reality that the different confessions and church legislations developed specific schools of theological thought, specific traditions, specific types of spirituality and even specific cultures. As a result, the ecumenical movement faces not only theological and ecclesiological divergences among the confessions but also divergent Christian life-styles – which may well constitute the major obstacle on the road towards unity.

2. The Orthodox community of faith

The Orthodox church calls itself the Orthodox-Catholic Church and understands itself as identical with the unique, authentic, undivided church which has preserved the pure and orthodox doctrine throughout the centuries to the present day. Consequently, a Christian who lives outside the Orthodox community does not share the full Christian truth. As the authentic and undivided church, the Orthodox community is believed to have come into existence together with the New Testament. The Orthodox church is made up of autocephalous churches. These are regional or national independent churches which may differ in theological emphases.

The Roman Catholic Church separated in 1054 from the true, Orthodox church. According to the Orthodox view, the Western church erroneously introduced papal primacy and an hierarchical constitution, while the Orthodox church preserved its essentially collegial, conciliar and democratic nature, expressed in local, provincial and national churches under the leadership of bishops and patriarchs, collegially governed by synods and councils.

For the Orthodox community Scripture and Tradition are the sources of doctrine and faith. According to its self-understanding,

> there is a living continuity between the apostolic community of the early church and the community that succeeds to it until the present day. The same faith, teachings, doctrine and Christian life continue to be present and perpetuate themselves throughout the history of the church. In this sense, the church continues to be apostolic, that is, in living continuity with the early Christian, apostolic community. Tradition, as the life of the church, is seen in terms of this living community with our Christian origins.[6]

The confession of faith of the Orthodox community is the Nicene Creed. Its trinitarian elements are supplemented with the Christology formulated at the Council of Constantinople.

The Orthodox dogmatic Tradition is limited to the seven oldest Ecumenical Councils (Nicea I in 325 to Nicea II in 787) and the Greek fathers of the patristic era. The general opinion, drawing on a canon of the sixth Ecumenical Council (680-681), is that "in interpreting Scriptures one should not hold other views than those expressed by 'the lights of the Church'. It is better to remain with their views to avoid difficulties and deviations."

Nicea is seen as the first and most important Ecumenical Council, with the later ones, including the Council of Constantinople, providing additions or explanations of the doctrinal and disciplinary texts of Nicea. Because of Nicea's emphasis on the Holy Trinity, the specific characteristic of Orthodox Tradition, doctrine and faith may be seen as their trinitarian emphasis.

The Holy Trinity is above all the object of adoration. The Triune God is and remains a mystery which neither the early Ecumenical Councils nor the fathers of the patristic era tried to fathom. The nature of the Triune God can never be adequately known or explained. God does not reveal his nature, but only its "surroundings". Orthodox theology and spirituality thus have an outspoken transcendental character. Knowledge of God can only be obtained through mystical experience and nourished by the sacraments, doctrine and witness. The foundation of this specific knowledge is the creation of the human person in God's image and likeness. Hence the emphasis of Orthodox spirituality on prayer, meditation and contemplation.

Tradition and the fathers of the patristic era speak extensively about the Holy Spirit. Orthodox theology in this connection underlines the specificity of the three persons: the Father, characterized by "unbornness", is called the source of divinity; the specificity of the Son is being born from the Father; that of the Spirit is being sent by the Father.

The Reformation attached great importance to the Orthodox trinitarian doctrine. The Reformers were convinced that in reacting against the degenerate church of the late Middle Ages, their movement was a continuation of the early church; and Luther and Calvin underlined the decisive relevance of the original confessions of faith. However, the Orthodox doctrine of the Trinity differs from the trinitarian theology in the West, which is more concerned with the action of the Trinity in the economy of salvation and in the history of humankind and the world.

Drawing on a New Testament reference to human persons as "partakers of the divine nature" (2 Pet. 1:14), Orthodox theology emphasizes the word and concept of *theosis* or "deification". Athanasius affirmed that "Christ did not become God from being human, but he became human from being God, in order to make us gods."[7] This objective ontological reality must permeate the human person and be realized subjectively.

Orthodox theology has always devoted substantial attention to cosmology, recognizing that the entire creation has a spiritual dimension. In recent years, appreciation for this spiritual dimension of creation has been recovered in the Western world as well, partly as a result of the ecumenical reflections around the WCC's conciliar process on Justice, Peace and the Integrity of Creation, to which Orthodox theologians made significant contributions.[8] One prominent expression of the spiritual dimension of creation can be found in the symbolism of icons, which are inherent to Orthodox religious culture. These religious paintings forge a link between the reality of this world and divine reality, a mirror of the religious dimension of God. As such, they represent supernatural reality.

Over the centuries, the Western confessions of faith have lost important characteristics which continue to be living realities in the East – among them the fascination exercised by the nature of God, the mystery of God's divine essence and mystical experience, as well as the influence on humankind and the whole of creation exercised by the incarnation of Jesus Christ, the Son sent by the Father. While the main points of the Christian confession of faith are identical in the East and in the West, the accents are different, due to historical developments that have created in distinct forms of confessional cultures and life-styles.

3. The Roman Catholic community of faith

The Roman Catholic Church recognizes the Apostles' Creed, the Nicene Creed, the Nicene-Constantinopolitan Creed and the Athanasian

Creed, which appear in sacramental and liturgical books, as authentic sources of the confession of faith. The Creed of the Council of Trent, published in 1564 as a reaction against the Reformation, contains a summary of the doctrines which Catholics are to believe.[9] In addition, a *Catechism of the Council of Trent,* written by Charles Borromeus and revised by Pope Pius V, was published in 1566.[10] Intended to instruct the clergy on Catholic doctrine, including the teaching of the Council of Trent, this catechism was for several centuries the classic handbook of Catholic religion, used by clergy, laity, Catholic families and training centres. Summaries of the catechism were obligatory material in Catholic schools. Later editions included definitions of the dogmas of the immaculate conception (1854), the papal infallibility (1870) and the assumption into heaven of the Mother of God (1950).

In 1992 Pope John Paul II approved the text of a new *Catechism of the Catholic Church,* containing "the faith of the Church and the Catholic doctrine testified or explained by Holy Scriptures, the apostolic tradition and the ecclesiastical magisterium... After the new codification of Canon Law of the Latin Church and the Canons of the Oriental Catholic Churches, the catechism offers an important contribution to the work of the renewal of the entire ecclesial life as willed and applied by the Second Vatican Council."[11]

The new Code of Canon Law, published in 1983, not only translates Catholic faith into juridical canons but also includes dogmatic and ecclesiastical formulations concerning the papacy, primacy, infallibility and the magisterium of the pope and the bishops, as well as moral and spiritual exhortations. Moreover, the new *Profession of Faith,* issued by the Congregation for the Doctrine of the Faith and approved by the Apostolic See in 1989, restates the Nicene-Constantinopolitan Creed and adds that a Catholic, besides accepting everything proposed by the Church as definite concerning faith and morals, "should adhere with religious submission... to the teachings which either the Roman pontiff or the college of bishops enunciate when they exercise their authentic magisterium, even if they do not intend to proclaim these teachings by a definite act".[12]

The differences between the Roman Catholic Church and the churches of the Reformation may be characterized in terms of their approaches to word and sacrament. To put it simply, Protestants base their faith on *Word*-revelation, while Roman Catholics believe in a *reality*-revelation, which comprises the mystery of Jesus Christ, the church and the sacraments. The fundamental design of the Roman Catholic community of faith lies in the elevation of the human being to supernatural perfection, the vision of the Triune God and sharing in God's nature.

The starting point of Roman Catholic theology is creation, specifically the creation of Adam. God endowed Adam with a body and an immortal soul, with reason and morality. He also gave him justice and holiness (called the *donum superadditum*). With original sin, this primordial sense of justice and holiness was lost. The way to human salvation aims at regaining these divine gifts and restoring communion with God. Here is a clear-cut distinction between nature and supernature as two distinct entities. The Council of Trent taught that justification, the recovery of justice and holiness, is a gratuitous act of God. Roman Catholic theology distinguishes at this point between the image of God and his likeness (Gen. 1). *Likeness* with God is the only foundation on which "children of God" (John 1:12) and "partakers of the divine nature" (2 Pet. 1:4) can become a reality.

Original sin is thus understood as the privation of the divine gifts and loss of the supernature. A first step towards regaining supernatural status can be taken with the help of the *gratia actualis*, which assists in beginning the process of justification. It is a call from God, as the Council of Trent states. *Gratia habitualis* then sustains this process, which can be lost through sin.

Regaining and maintaining primordial justice, holiness and *gratia habitualis* require the means of salvation of the Roman Catholic Church: the sacraments of baptism and penance. Since the life of the Catholic believer is interwoven from birth to death with the sacraments, especially baptism and the confession of sins, the Roman Catholic Church, which is free to administer or refuse the sacraments, exercises absolute authority and power over the faithful.

Two old sayings – "Where grace is, there is the Church" and "Where the pope is, there is the Church" – are equally important for the Roman Catholic Church. The tension between faith understood as charism and the institutional elements of the Church of Rome has often been noted. Certainly the elements pertaining to faith are completely embedded in the institutional constellation, since the Roman Catholic Church is first and foremost a hierarchical institution in which all immediate power is concentrated in the person of the bishop of Rome. He alone governs the church, with the help of and in communion with the bishops he appoints, and through the Roman Curia. As the *Code of Canon Law* puts it: "The Supreme Pontiff usually conducts the business of the universal Church by means of the Roman Curia, which fulfills its duty in his name and by his authority, for the good and the service of the churches" (Canon 360). From the time of the Reformation to the present day, the Roman pontiff, together with the various departments of the Roman Curia, has issued innumerable documents on faith and morals. As a result, the Catholic community of faith knows exactly what to believe and how to behave. The certainty of being saved is absolute. Significantly, the *Code of Canon Law* neither regulates the work of the Roman Curia nor indicates any limitation of its authority.

For centuries, the Roman Catholic Church and the Catholic community of faith were closed systems. Communication with other Christian churches was seen as unnecessary, something to be avoided, even heretical. The Second Vatican Council was an occasion for the Church of Rome to open up to other Christian churches and to the world. This came to the fore in new official collaboration with the non-Roman Catholic churches. This official ecumenism, however, is not the same as the ecumenical spirit that animates the Catholic community of faith. Ecumenism in the believing community is often far ahead of the official church in its efforts to break the barriers that still exist among Christians.

4. The Lutheran community of faith

From the outset, the Reformation introduced the Apostles' Creed, the Nicene Creed and the Nicene-Constantinopolitan Creed as the theological foundation and norm for the faith (*norma normata*), in addition to Scripture. They were considered to make an important link with the faith of the early church, and in this way to show that the Reformation was a continuation of the apostolic church. Luther's catechisms and the Augsburg Confession refer explicitly to these texts as guidelines for the new Reformation theology and church legislation.[13]

The specific Lutheran confessions of faith are assembled in the *Book of Concord* (1580). In addition to the Augsburg Confession (1530), which the Lutheran community of faith has considered for more than four-and-a-half centuries as the authentic source of its confession, this contains the two catechisms written by Luther (1529), the Schmalkaldian Articles (1537), Melanchthon's *De potestate et primatu Papae*, and a *Collection of Testimonies*, which are quotations from the patristic era. The *Book of Concord* is the official doctrinal corpus of Lutheran churches.

For the Reformers, the question of justification is the core of Christian faith, a global principle "which serves to interpret the entire gamut of doctrines and practices that go to make up the Christian whole: God's saving action, the reality and life of Jesus Christ, the practice and action of the church, especially in its sacraments and preaching, Christian anthropology, spirituality and ethics".[14]

For Luther, everything begins and ends with God's free, merciful and gracious initiative, grasped and lived by the human being. The subject of theology is *homo peccator* and *Deus iustificans* – the human being as sinner and the justifying God. As he tried to understand Paul's Epistle to the Romans, Luther wrote,

> nothing stood in the way but that one expression, the "justice of God" (Rom. 1:17), because I took it to mean that justice whereby God is just and deals justly in punishing the unjust. My situation was that, although an impeccable monk, I stood before God as a sinner troubled in conscience, and I had no confidence that my merit would please him. Therefore I did not love a just and angry God, but rather hated and murmured against him. Yet I clung to dear Paul and had a great yearning to know what he meant... Night and day I pondered until I saw the connection between the justice of God and the statement that "the just shall live by faith" (Rom. 1:17). Then I grasped that the justice of God is that right-eousness by which through grace and sheer mercy God justifies us through faith. Thereupon I felt myself to be reborn and to have gone through open doors into paradise. The whole of Scripture took on a new meaning, and whereas before the "justice of God" had filled me with hate, now it became to me inex-pressibly sweet in greater love. The passage of Paul became a gate to heaven.[15]

Righteousness or justice is a gift from God which the human person accepts in faith, joy and gratitude, without any need for preliminary or preparatory works. God makes the sinner just. The righteousness of God – God's active, unconditional mercy towards the sinner – is revealed and made present in Christ, especially on the cross. Christ's action and life are one and the same thing as God's outgoing, justifying self-giving. Thus, the life of a Christian is one of dynamic interchange with God, centred in and made possible by the life and action of Christ the Saviour, God and man, who has become our justice before God.[16]

When Luther speaks of *faith alone,* he is underscoring the exclusion of works. Faith itself is not a human work but God's own gift. It is the specific way in which Christ – and God with Christ – is present in the human person. Human persons are justified not so much on account of their faith, but on account of Christ. The justice received is not our own, and our faith is perfect only because of Christ. The concepts *solus Deus, sola gratia, solus Christus, sola fides* mean that only God makes a per-son just, that justice is God's gift alone, and that this gift is identified with the life and action of Jesus Christ; the human acceptance of that gift is exclusively God's work.[17]

Luther's frequent statement that justification is entirely outside us may seem to contradict his affirmation that the new justified life is our true life. But what he really means is that our new, justified and redeemed life is in Christ. The human person lives in Christ: "it is no longer I who live but Christ who lives in me" (Gal. 2:20). By believing, the human being forms a unity with Christ. In faith we are able to con-template God's justice in us. Righteousness is not a personal possession but something outside of and attributed to the human person.

So strongly did Luther emphasize that works are useless for salvation that he has sometimes been interpreted as affirming either that persons sin in everything they do or that Christians cannot sin, no matter what their behaviour.

> This paradoxical and at times contradictory way of speaking about sin and grace, very characteristic of Luther, must be understood in its context. In fact it reflects a living or existential dialectic at the very heart of his teachings, that may be expressed succinctly in his famous phrases, "sin and sin boldly", and, in particular, *homo simul iustus et peccator*.[18]

According to Luther, human beings are "constitutionally" sinners. Whatever we do, we sin, and sin gravely. Yet the Christ who has come in us moves us to live a new life, and in doing so we are in the process of being gradually healed, redeemed and sanctified.

Justification is the truth about the relationship between God and the human person. Thus, it is the foundation for considering all theological issues. The relationship between law and gospel is marked by justification. The law is a qualification of human existence before any reference to the gospel is made. "The law accuses," Luther wrote. It reveals the real meaning of original sin. In fulfilling the law, the human being is not justified. The Augsburg Confession, reflecting Luther's concept of canon law, says explicitly that there is no relation between church order and salvation. Church legislation is made to promote peace and right order in the church. The human person certainly needs the law, but only *after* justification. Under the law – that is, before justification – human beings on their own are obliged to obey, but they cannot achieve perfection. Under the gospel, however, the human person, being saved and justified, "is promised that Christ has died for him and taken on his guilt. Christ's righteousness becomes his own; the believer is transplanted from himself into Christ..., so that Christ himself becomes the new being of the sinner. He is justified in his relationship to God, and sinner according to his own quality (*simul iustus et peccator*)."[19]

In the broad sense, justification and the gospel are related not only to the individual person but also have relevance for the ordering of the world. While Luther's doctrine of the "two kingdoms" is generally associated with the relationship between church and state, subsequent developments have moved from an exclusive concentration on the spiritual and temporal spheres to the human being created by God as a whole. The body is an essential part of the human person; salvation promised in Jesus Christ relates to the whole human being; and every Christian has a social and communitarian dimension. Here moral and ethical dimensions come to the fore.

Finally, the doctrine of the two kingdoms points to establishing the reign of Christ on earth. The two kingdoms are both parallel to and completely different from one another, recalling again the dialectics of *simul iustus et peccator*. A contemporary interpretation of Luther's doctrine of the two kingdoms can be found in the theological statement of the Barmen Synod (1934), signed by representatives of both the Lutheran and the Reformed communities of faith.[20]

5. The Reformed community of faith

With some reservations, John Calvin considered the Apostles' Creed, the Nicene-Constantinopolitan Creed and the Athanasian Creed as authentic sources of the Christian faith. Unlike the Lutherans, his followers did not establish an official collection of confessions of faith, but the Reformed community considered the following documents, supplemented by a few local or regional texts, to contain genuine sources of its faith: Calvin's Catechism of the Church of Geneva (1545), the confession of faith of the French Reformed Churches, also called the Confession of La Rochelle (1563), the Canons of the Synod of Dordrecht (1619) and – primarily in the Anglo-Saxon world – the Westminster Confession (1645).

The Reformers' views on authority, papacy and primacy led them to reflect anew on the nature and role of the church. Quite understandably, they sought to avoid any characteristics inherent in the hierarchical system. Thus Calvin's Catechism of the Church of Geneva says that the church is the "body and society of believers whom God has predestined to eternal life",[21] and the Second Helvetic Confession defines the church as

> a company of the faithful called and gathered out of the world; a communion of all saints, that is, of them who truly know and rightly worship and serve the true God, in Jesus Christ the Saviour, by the word and the Holy Spirit, and who by faith are partakers of all those good graces which are freely offered through Jesus Christ (Art. 17).[22]

In sum, the confessions of the Reformed community teach that the church is the assembly or congregation of believers. It is Christ who gathers the believers. The believers must respond to the call of Christ by gathering together. Christ is the Head, and he assembles, protects and sustains the congregation by his Spirit and word.

Despite the aversion of the Reformers and their followers to institutionalism, congregations had to be organized, ministers had to follow certain rules, members had to live according to a certain discipline. Right from the beginning the Reformation introduced a certain juridical practice which later developed into a complex of rules and prescriptions called "church order".

The Confession of the Reformed Churches of France affirms that church order, which has been authoritatively established, must be believed as sacred and inviolable. Moreover, the church cannot exist without pastors, whose duty is to teach and who should be listened to with reverence when they are exercising their ministry. This is not to say that God depends on these helpers, but it pleases him to maintain them under such a charge. To the extent that they live with illusions, it is up to them to reduce these and to preach the word of God and administer the sacraments.[23]

The church is also described in the Reformed confessions as the congregation of those who look to Jesus Christ for their salvation. The congregation is where the word is proclaimed and the Lord's supper is celebrated. Its government does not come from outside – from Rome or anywhere else – but from within the congregation. The nature of church government is clearly described with an appeal to the gospel. The way in which the church is governed should be spiritual. The poor and distressed must be helped and consoled; transgressors and dissenters must be warned and corrected in this same spirit. The Reformed community put a great emphasis on discipline in the life of the congregation, including individual moral behaviour – even considering discipline as a characteristic "mark of the church".

The Heidelberg Catechism (1563) states that

> According to the command of Christ, those who, though called Christians, profess un-Christian teachings or live un-Christian lives, and after repeated and loving counsel refuse to abandon their errors and wickedness, and after being reported to the church, that is, to its officers, fail to respond also to their admonition – such persons the officers exclude from the Christian fellowship by withholding the sacraments from them, and God himself excludes them from the kingdom of Christ. Such persons, when promising and demonstrating genuine reform, are received again as members of Christ and of his church (Q.&A. 84).

From the outset there was diversity in structures of government among the churches of the Reformation. The Anglican Church preserved the episcopacy, as did the Lutheran churches. While a few Reformed churches – in Hungary, for example – have bishops, the majority of them emphasized that Christ as the one head of the church is the unique and general bishop. The question of the episcopal function was thus for the most part considered irrelevant within the Reformed churches.

Having rejected the Roman Catholic view of the predominant role of the church as sacramental institution of salvation, the Reformers had to look elsewhere to emphasize both the fact that sinners have no way in themselves alone to reach salvation and God's initiative to offer grace. For Calvin, the answer was election out of pure grace, whereas for Luther, as we have seen, it was the doctrine of justification. Consequently, the doctrine of predestination came to characterize the Reformed community of faith. After Calvin, the main locus of this teaching was the Canons of the Synod of Dordrecht (1619).

In Roman Catholic doctrine, the relationship between God and the human person starts with creation. The long way from original sin to the final goal of the *visio Dei* leads via the reception of the first grace, the habitual grace, the sacraments administered by the church, and the collaboration with grace by means of good works and merits, to permanent supernatural life and final communion with God in the *visio beata*. The Reformation understands the relationship between God and the human person as beginning not with creation but with the fall and original sin, which fatefully mark the human person. Thus the Catholic schema of "creation-nature-grace" is replaced by "sin-grace". In the words of Calvin, God himself had to come to move the human person out of his nature. This sombre view of human nature is the background to the Reformed confessions, treatment of original sin, the corruption of human nature and its natural culpability. This also explains the influence of the role of Jesus Christ as Redeemer and Saviour on the anthropology and ecclesiology of the Reformation. Rather than the Roman Catholic *ubi gratia* or *ubi papa, ibi ecclesia*, what is essential for the Reformation is *ubi Christus, ibi ecclesia:* where Christ is, there the church is.

Communion with Jesus Christ is the core of the Reformed confessions of faith. But while Luther dislodged justification from the human person's long journey towards God, Calvin disconnected election from God's providence. In effect, these two priorities, justification and election, have almost never been harmoniously lived. The impression is that in the Lutheran confession election was hidden behind justification, and that the Reformed confession concealed justification from election.

The Confession of Faith of the Reformed Churches of France affirms that all human beings are affected by general corruption and condemnation. But God's goodness and mercy in Jesus Christ has elected some from all eternity, without taking into consideration their good works. To manifest his justice, he leaves the others to their corruption and condemnation.[24] The Second Helvetic Confession also refers explicitly to the predestination from all eternity of the saints whom God wants to save in Jesus Christ. God has chosen them in Christ and out of love for Christ, while those who are outside Christ are rejected.

The Synod of Dordrecht affirms that God elects whom he wants to elect when he wishes. Election calls the chosen ones "to repentance and faith in Christ crucified" (Art. 3). As for the faith God gives to some and not to others, this depends on his eternal decree. Election proceeds from God's will and God's grace (Art. 7). "Just as God himself is most wise, unchangeable, all-knowing, and almighty, so the election made by him can neither be suspended nor altered, revoked, or annulled; neither can his chosen ones be cast off, nor their number reduced" (Art. 11).

6. The Anglican community of faith

The Anglican community confesses the Apostles' Creed, the Nicene-Constantinopolitan Creed and the Athanasian Creed, and acknowledges the *Thirty-Nine Articles* as the authentic document of its belief. All of these are found in the *Book of Common Prayer,* which thus in the broad sense also belongs to the confession of the Anglican faith.

The Anglican Church comprises a great number of churches. The Church of England is divided into two provinces, Canterbury and York. The archbishop of Canterbury is *primus inter pares.* Both provinces celebrate convocations, comparable to provincial synods, attended by bishops, members of the clergy and representatives of the universities. For the whole country, general synods of the Church of England are convoked, which are also attended by the laity. Every ten years, the Lambeth Conference brings together the bishops of all the Anglican churches around the world to study themes of current interest. Furthermore, an Anglican Consultative Council advises on more important issues. In order to develop and maintain positive contacts with all Christian churches and communities, the Anglican Church gives high priority to dialogues with other Christian churches.

A number of characteristic features of the Anglican community of faith may be mentioned:

1. The Anglican community is part of the Reformation. From the outset it rejected the doctrinal "errors" of the Roman Catholic Church and its canon law. Instead of the Roman pontiff, the English sovereign became the supreme head of the *Ecclesia Anglicana.*

2. Some Anglican doctrines were formulated according to the example of the Lutheran church; for other doctrinal themes, such as predestination and the Lord's supper, elements from Calvinistic teachings have been integrated into the *corpus doctrinae.*

3. In state-church relationships the ecclesiastical government is subordinated to the secular power.

4. The traditional episcopal institution has been maintained as an essential element of the Anglican spirit. This has led to the conviction

that Anglicanism has an intermediary function between the Roman Catholic Church, the Orthodox churches and the churches of the Reformation. The Anglican emphasis on the early sources of Christianity can also be understood in this context.

5. The fact that both the *Thirty-Nine Articles* and the *Book of Common Prayer* belong to the confession of the Anglican community of faith and the inclusion in Anglican canon law of so many different elements may be seen in terms of what Anglicans understand as a widening of the "doctrinal church" to the "comprehensive church".

The *Thirty-Nine Articles of Religion* are preceded by a declaration of His Majesty as "Supreme Governor of the Church within our Dominion".[25] After several articles dealing with the Holy Trinity, Article 6 states that Holy Scripture "contains all things necessary to salvation". The succeeding articles mention the three creeds of the early church, which "ought thoroughly to be received and believed; for they may be proved by most certain warrants of Holy Scripture".

In dealing with "original or birth sin", the *Thirty-Nine Articles* follow the Reformers:

> Every person born into the world deserves God's wrath and damnation..., and his condition is such that he cannot turn and prepare himself by his own natural strength and good works to faith and calling upon God... We are accounted righteous before God only for the merit of our Lord and Saviour Jesus Christ by faith and not for our own works or deservings. Good works are the fruits of faith and follow after justification... They are pleasing and acceptable to God in Christ and do spring out necessarily of a true and lively faith... After we have received the Holy Ghost, we may depart from grace given, and fall into sin, and by the grace of God we may arise again and amend our lives.

Article 17 affirms that "predestination to life is the everlasting purpose of God whereby he has constantly decreed by his counsel secret to us to deliver from curse and damnation those whom he has chosen in Christ out of mankind and to bring them by Christ to everlasting salvation".

With regard to the church and sacraments, the text reads:

> The visible church of Christ is a congregation of faithful men, in which the pure Word of God is preached and the sacraments be duly ministered... As the church of Jerusalem, Alexandria, and Antioch have erred, so also the Church of Rome has erred, not only in their living and manner of ceremonies, but also in matters of faith.
>
> The Romish doctrine concerning purgatory, pardons, worshippings and adoration, as well of images as of relics and also invocation of saints, is a fond thing vainly invented and grounded upon no warranty of Scripture, but rather repugnant to the Word of God.

There are two sacraments ordained of Christ our Lord in the Gospel, that is to say baptism and the supper of the Lord... Unworthiness of the ministers hinders not the effect of the sacraments.

Baptism is considered not only a sign of being Christian and belonging to the church but also of forgiveness of sin and adoption as children of God. "Faith is confirmed and grace increased by virtue of prayer unto God." In explaining the Lord's supper as the sacrament of our redemption by Christ's death, Article 28 asserts that the Roman Catholic doctrine of transubstantiation "cannot be proved by Holy Writ... The offering of Christ once made is that perfect redemption, propitiation and satisfaction for all the sins of the whole world." The idea that the sacrifices of masses give remission of pain or guilt is a "blasphemous fable and dangerous deceit".

The *Book of Common Prayer* offers general and specific norms for ceremonies, as well as special dates and times for reading the psalms and specific moments for Scripture reading. One part is devoted to daily prayers and prayers to be said at decisive moments of Christian life – including prayers for visiting the sick, travelling and facing threats due to the weather. The *Book of Common Prayer* thus offers a manual for living one's life in the presence of God.

7. The common faith: a process of discovery

The way in which the various confessions of faith consciously drew confessional boundaries to insulate themselves from the influence of the other communities of faith is set in sharp relief by the distance the Orthodox churches and the Roman Catholic Church kept from the emerging confessional families. Each of them claims to be the only true church of Jesus Christ. The Roman Catholic Church consciously isolated itself by condemning the members of all other churches as heretics or schismatics.

As each confession elaborated its own specific identity, its differences from other confessions were emphasized. These specific identities resulted in different confessional cultures. In Europe, where religion was for centuries a highly important element in the individual and social spheres, different confessional cultures produced different life-styles among the members of the various confessions. The daily life of Protestants was marked by their church affiliation. Doctrinal differences – however insignificant in reality – were translated into diversities of lifestyle and everyday behaviour.

The Anglican community, with its *Thirty-Nine Articles* – and more specifically its attempt to find the "intermediary way" – can be seen as a first attempt to synthesize elements from the confessions of faith of the

Reformation. The Anglican community of faith confesses and harmoniously lives doctrinal teachings of both the Lutheran and the Calvinist traditions.

When church legislation and church law became a prominent subject of research and study among Protestant scholars in Germany at the beginning of the 19th century, it became apparent that differences in faith convictions between Lutherans and Reformed were not so important as had been believed in the 16th and 17th centuries, that traditional life-styles had grown further apart than doctrinal issues. Especially in regions where members of both traditions lived together, the awareness that peripheral matters were more divisive than fundamental faith convictions made it possible for unions between Lutheran and Reformed to emerge without great difficulty:

> Such a true religious union of both Protestant churches which are divided only in exterior differences is in conformity with the very aim of Christianity. It is in agreement with the first goals of the Reformation. It is in accordance with the Protestant spirit, promotes the familiarity with the church and is salvific for family piety. It will be of help for the improvement of churches and schools which were hampered by the division of the confessions.[26]

While the unions between Lutheran and Calvinist churches in the first half of the 19th century were of some practical value in church-state relationships, their primary importance lay in the theoretical and practical encounter between the two traditions, which meant a liberation from traditional oppositions. In this new spirit, common church legislations and church laws were elaborated, and common synods were celebrated or developed new forms, with more lay attendance.

During this period, the churches also began to work out church constitutions. In marking the boundaries between the competences of church and state, these promoted a process that would finally lead to the separation of the church from a secularized state. Especially in the case of the Lutheran churches, this meant breaking with the traditional church-state affinity. This evolution aroused great interest among church lawyers, among them R. Sohm, who went so far as to state that church law is a denial of the very nature of the church.

The theological statement of the Confessing Church in Germany at the Synod of Barmen (1934) contained six theses formulating the faith of Christianity and the Reformation over against the Nazi claims on the church. As such it was a genuine confession of faith. Particularly significant was the fact that it was the fruit of close collaboration between representatives of the Lutheran and Reformed churches. The work of members of the Confessing Church in German-occupied countries – the

Netherlands, Norway and France – led to the emergence of a European Confessing Church.

The Confessing Church has often been cited as a model for situations of sharp confrontation between church and state and severe political oppression. The Barmen Declaration became a model statement of Christian freedom, inspiring many texts and documents with a common input by Christians of different denominations.

Among the notable 20th-century achievements between the two mainline Reformation families, the most impressive is perhaps the Leuenberg Agreement (1973), for which a number of post-war national dialogues had paved the way. One of these, in 1957, formulated the Arnoldshain theses, which state that the New Testament provides no jus- tification for the eucharistic division of the traditional confessions. The critical text at Leuenberg was Article 7 of the Augsburg Confession, which affirms that for "the true unity of the church it is enough to agree concerning the teaching of the gospel and the administration of the sacraments". The common faith of the Reformation churches – the cen- trality of justification by faith for the preaching, teaching and sacramen- tal life of the church – was underlined. The 16th-century condemnations, especially those concerning the Lord's supper, were lifted as unjustified. Churches which sign the Leuenberg Agreement declare that they are in full communion, that is, in table and pulpit fellowship. By the end of the 1980s, some 80 churches had signed the agreement.

The international Lutheran-Reformed dialogue in 1985 decided that the mutual condemnations of the past no longer applied and that the diversities between the two traditions are in the context of unity on fun- damental issues. Thus it recommended pulpit and table fellowship and growth together in mission.[27] That same year a dialogue began between the Protestant churches in what was then a divided Germany and the Church of England. This culminated in January 1991 with the signing of the Meissen Statement, which recognizes both as churches in which the word of God is authentically proclaimed and the sacraments properly administered. The ministries of the churches are recognized and eucharistic hospitality recommended. The statement also expressed the hope that doctrinal divergences will soon be resolved.

The Porvoo Statement of October 1992 between the Church of Eng- land and the Nordic Lutheran churches expresses a common under- standing of the mission and faith of the church. One chapter deals with "the episcopate in service of the apostolicity of the church". Like the 1974 Anglican-Lutheran Niagara Statement, Porvoo affirms that indi- vidual and collegial episcopé is exercised in the churches in a multiplic- ity of forms, in continuity with the apostolic life, the apostolic mission and the apostolic office. The office of episcopé is exercised in the person of the bishop who in the historic succession is ordained with the imposition of the hands. The Porvoo Common Statement does not exclusively recognize the episcopé in the form of bishops, but equally acknowledges the "presbyterial" form of this office.

NOTES

[1] Documentary History of Faith and Order 1963-1993, pp.29-30.

[2] David Paton ed., *Breaking Barriers, Nairobi 1975: Official Report of the Fifth Assembly of the WCC*, Geneva, WCC Publications, 1976, SPCK, p.66.

[3] The study process is documented in the following WCC Faith and Order publications: *Towards a Confession of the Common Faith* (Faith and Order Paper no. 100, 1980); *Towards Visible Unity*, F&O Paper no. 113, (1982); *Apostolic Faith Today: A Handbook for Study*, (F&O Paper no. 124, 1985); *Confessing One Faith: Towards an Ecumenical Explication of the Apostolic Faith as Expressed in the Nicene-Constantinopolitan Creed* (F&O Paper no. 140, 1987); *Confessing the One Faith: An Ecumenical Explication of the Apostolic Faith as it is Confessed in the Nicene-Constantinopolitan Creed* (F&O Paper no. 153, 1991).

[4] Michael Kinnamon, ed., *Signs of the Spirit: Official Report of the Seventh Assembly of the WCC*, Geneva, WCC Publications, 1991, p.174.

[5] Cf. G. P. Hartvelt, *Symboliek: een beschrijving van kernen van christelijk belijden*, Kampen, Kok, 1991.

[6] Maximos Aghiorgousis, "The Dogmatic Tradition of the Orthodox Church", in Litsas, ed., *A Companion to the Greek Orthodox Church*, pp.18-19.

[7] G. P. Hartelt, *op. cit.* p.49.

[8] Cf. Marc Reuver, "The People of God and the Conciliar Process", in D. Preman Niles, ed., *Between the Flood and the Rainbow*, Geneva, WCC Publications, 1992, pp.26-33.

[9] For the text see Denzinger, Eng. tr., pp.6-9.

[10] *Catéchisme du Concile de Trente*, Bouère, France, Editions Dominique Martin Morin, repr. 1984.

[11] Quoted from the Apostolic Constitution *Fidei Depositum*, Catéchisme de l'Eglise catholique, p.8.

[12] *Acta Apostolicae Sedis*, 81, 1989, 104-106; cf. Canon 833; Pope John Paul II, Apostolic Letter *Ad Tuendam Fidem*, in L' *Osservatore Romano*, English ed., 15 July 1998; Congregation for the Doctrine of the Faith, *Doctrinal Commentary on Concluding Formula of "Professio Fidei"*.

[13] H. Dombois, *Das Recht der Gnade*, Witten, Luther Verlag, 1961, Vol. 1, pp.677-705.

[14] Paul O'Callaghan, *Fides Christi: The Justification Debate*, Portland, Four Courts Press, 1997, pp.19-20.

[15] *Werke*, WA, 54, 185f.

[16] Paul O'Callaghan, *op. cit.*, pp.25-27.

[17] *Ibid.*, pp.28-31.

[18] *Ibid.*, p.35.

[19] D. Lange, in *Lutheran Quarterly*, 1991; quoted by O'Callaghan, *ibid.*, pp.229f.

[20] Cf. Albert Stein, "Herrschaft Christi und geschwisterliche Gemeinde", in Rau, et al., eds, *Das Recht der Kirche*, Vol. II. pp.272-317.

[21] English text in J.K.S. Reid, ed., *Calvin: Theological Treatises*, p.102.

[22] Text in John H. Leith, ed., *Creeds of the Churches*, Atlanta, John Knox, 3d ed., 1982, p.141.

[23] Text in Olivier Fatio, ed., *Confessions et Catéchismes de la foi réformée*, Geneva, Labor et Fides, 1986, p.123.

[24] *Ibid.*, p.119.

[25] Text from Cajus Fabricius, ed., *Die Kirche von England, Ihr Gebetbuch, Bekenntnis und Kanonisches Recht*, pp.374-402.

[26] Quoted by Joachim Mehlhausen, "Kirche zwischen Staat und Gesellschaft", in *Das Recht der Kirche*, Vol. II, p.217.

[27] G. Schieffer, *Von Schauenburg Nach Leuenberg: Entstehung und Bedeutung der Konkordie reformatorischer Kirchen in Europa*, Paderborn, Bonifacius, 1982.

CHAPTER 5

The Churches and Ecumenism

1. A variety of churches

The WCC's Commission on Faith and Order observed at its meeting in Stavanger, Norway, in 1985, that

> in a divided Christianity, the existing churches come to their reflection and tasks with varying understandings of the nature, identity and boundaries of the church. The churches' differences come to expression in several ways: their perceptions of the character of the church as both the body and bride of Christ and a historic human reality; the role they attribute to the institutional element that is necessary to any form of ecclesial life; the place they recognize to the church in the saving activity of God; the sense in which the church itself may be said to be sacramental in character; the weight they attach to ecclesiology in their doctrinal schemes. Most concretely, the existing churches differ as to the persons and communities which are to be reckoned as belonging to the church.[1]

British Methodist theologian and ecumenist Geoffrey Wainwright has worked out an historical and systematic typology of existing ecclesiologies – the differing perceptions of the identity, nature, unity and mission of the church which have emerged over the centuries and are still present in our days.[2] As a consequence of the increasing importance of ecumenism, however, some of the boundaries between different concepts of the church are beginning to vanish.

In the understanding originating from Cyprian of Carthage in the 3rd century, there exists only one church, whose institutional and spiritual boundaries coincide. One becomes a member of this church through baptism; and anyone who falls into heresy (failure of faith) or schism (failure of love) lacks the Holy Spirit and falls into an ecclesial void. The Orthodox belief remains closest to this concept of the church. According to its ecclesiology the Orthodox church is the one true church of Christ. Being his body, it is not and cannot be divided. This one church is a direct testimony of God's self-giving love to his undivided church. There is no movement towards unity; the very existence of the church derives from the inseparable union between the three persons of the Holy Trinity, given to humankind as a historical event on the day of Pentecost.

According to a view attributed to Augustine, the church coincides with those who are baptized in the name of the Father, Son and Holy Spirit. Historically, the Augustinian position is characteristic of the Church of Rome. The Council of Trent – which stated that baptism administered by heretics is valid – also decreed that "if anyone says that it is not according to the institution of Christ our Lord himself, that is by divine law, that St Peter has perpetual successors in the primacy over the whole Church, or if anyone says that the Roman Pontiff is not the successor of St Peter in the same primacy: let him be anathema".[3] Here the Council was reaffirming the statement of Pope Boniface VIII in the bull *Unam Sanctam* that "it is absolutely necessary for the salvation of every human creature to be subject to the Roman pontiff".[4] Like the Orthodox church, the Roman Catholic Church claims to be the only true church of Jesus Christ: "This Church, constituted and organized as a society in the present world, subsists in the Catholic Church."[5]

Luther and Calvin made a clear distinction between the visible church on earth and the hidden, invisible church of all those who are "justified" or "elect" by a free act of God. The visible church on earth is first and foremost a local church. Article 8 of the *Augsburg Confession* declares: "The church is a gathering of believers in which the gospel is purely preached and the sacraments are administered according to the gospel." Lutherans are doctrinally and legally identified by the same confessions of faith. The Reformed churches, too, have a common set of confessions.

The Reformation also gave birth to territorial or particular churches, limited by both civil boundaries under the lordship of princes or kings and their confessional relation to either Lutheranism or Calvinism. The claim of the churches of the Reformation to confess the same faith as the church of the apostolic era is not intended to deny apostolicity to other Protestant or non-Protestant churches. God's grace is active in all Christian churches, but church unity does not have the same meaning for all Protestant churches. According to Article 7 of the Augsburg Confession, to bring about the unity of the church it is enough to reach convergence on the doctrine of the gospel and on the administration of the sacraments. To a great extent the Protestant Reformers abandoned hierarchical structures of the church in favour of local congregations or clusters of congregations governed by synods, understood as a continuation of the synodal praxis of the early centuries of Christianity.

Anglicanism in its early period was limited to the British Isles. It tried to make a synthesis of elements from Luther and Calvin with an hierarchical structure similar to that of the Orthodox church. The Anglican church considers itself a continuation of the apostolic church and strongly promotes the study of patristic theology. Its original institutional and spiritual boundaries coincided with those of Britain. The head of the *Ecclesia Anglicana* is the sovereign king or queen; and in England the Anglican church is the "national established church". Later, however, Anglicanism spread to the countries of the British Commonwealth as well as other parts of the world. In 1930 the Lambeth Conference described the Anglican Communion as it now exists as a fellowship within the one holy, catholic and apostolic church of those duly constituted dioceses, provinces or regional churches which are in communion with the see of Canterbury. These churches uphold and propagate the catholic and apostolic faith and order as generally set forth in the *Book of Common Prayer* and in the *Constitutions and Canons Ecclesiastical*. All this confronts the Anglican Communion with important questions of unity, identity and mission. The absence of a central decision-making office is seriously felt in doctrinal and practical matters. It might be said that within the Anglican Communion the charismatic element and the institutional element live alongside each other, sometimes in tension, sometimes in a kind of fusion, but seldom truly resolved.[6]

Traditionally, churches have been classified into two categories: universal churches and particular churches.[7] On the one side are the Orthodox church and the Roman Catholic Church, which claim confessional universality and a potential or actual worldwide dimension. On the other side are the particular churches, considered as limited to a specific confession and a defined geographical territory. The Orthodox church has equally emphasized the local and the universal elements.

2. A fellowship of local churches

Given their variety and the different emphases in their self-understanding, how can the churches move towards the goal of visible unity? The statements on the unity of the church approved by the assemblies of the World Council of Churches since its third assembly (New Delhi 1961) focus on the local church as the basic unit. The New Delhi assembly declared:

> We believe that the unity which is both God's will and his gift to his church is being made visible as all in each place who are baptized into Jesus Christ and confess him as Lord and Saviour are brought by the Holy Spirit into one fully committed fellowship, holding the one apostolic faith, preaching the one gospel, breaking the one bread, joining in common prayer, and having a corporate life reaching out in witness and service to all, and at the same time are united with the whole Christian fellowship in all places and all ages in such

wise that ministry and members are accepted by all, and that all can act and speak together as occasion requires for the task to which God calls his people.8

The fifth assembly of the WCC (Nairobi 1975) received and approved a recommendation of the Faith and Order Commission, formulated at its Salamanca conference (1973) which affirmed:

> The one church is to be envisioned as a conciliar fellowship of local churches which are themselves truly united. In this conciliar fellowship, each local church possesses, in communion with the others, the fullness of catholicity, witnesses to the same apostolic faith, and therefore recognizes the others as belonging to the same church of Christ and guided by the same Spirit. As the New Delhi assembly pointed out, they are bound together because they have received the same baptism and share in the same eucharist: they recognize each other's members and ministries. They are one in their common commitment to confess the gospel of Christ by proclamation and service to the world. To this end, each church aims at maintaining sustained and sustaining relationships with her sister churches, expressed in conciliar gatherings whenever required for the fulfilment of their common calling.9

The seventh assembly (Canberra 1991) emphasized the characteristic of communion, koinonia, of the fellowship of local churches:

> The purpose of God according to holy scripture is to gather the whole of creation under the Lordship of Christ Jesus in whom, by the power of the Holy Spirit, all are brought into communion with God (Eph. 1). The church is the foretaste of this communion with God and with one another. The grace of our Lord Jesus Christ, the love of God and the communion of the Holy Spirit enable the one church to live as sign of the reign of God and servant of the reconciliation with God, promised and provided for the whole creation. The purpose of the church is to unite people with Christ in the power of the Spirit, to manifest communion in prayer and action and thus to point to the fullness of communion with God, humanity and the whole creation in the glory of the kingdom...
>
> Because of sin and misunderstandings of the diverse gifts of the Spirit, the churches are painfully divided within themselves and among each other...
>
> We acknowledge with gratitude to God that in the ecumenical movement the churches walk together... This has allowed them to recognize a certain degree of communion already existing between them...
>
> The unity of the church to which we are called is a koinonia given and expressed in the common confession of the apostolic faith; a common sacramental life entered by the one baptism and celebrated together in one eucharistic fellowship; a common life in which members and ministries are mutually recognized and reconciled... The goal of the church for full communion is realized when all the churches are able to recognize in one another the one, holy, catholic and apostolic church in its fullness. This full communion will be expressed on the local and the universal levels through conciliar forms of life and action.10

The ecclesiological trend towards considering the local church as elementary and primary, reflected in the Nairobi assembly's definition of a "conciliar fellowship of local churches", quite naturally led to questions about the exact meaning of the term "local church". Studies and discussions by the Faith and Order Commission and the WCC sub-unit on Renewal and Congregational Life, including a consultation in Geneva in 1976, led to a document entitled *A Fellowship of Local Churches Truly United.*[11]

"Local church" has different meanings in the various confessional traditions. The geographical dimension of "local" can refer to a rather limited or a relatively large place. Theologically, the essential relatedness of the concept of the church to a place is part of the Christian tradition. Jean-Marie Tillard, in his extensive study of the local church, has documented this relatedness of the local church to a place – first to a city, as for example Jerusalem, later to a diocesan see. Scripture and patristic literature testify that these places had in common one and the same faith, the sacraments, especially baptism, and the eucharist. Tillard speaks of a "fraternal koinonia", a communion of local churches in which all of them, geographically small or large, possessed the fullness of the Spirit and together formed a real communion. Referring to the bishop who presides over the celebration of the eucharist, Tillard writes:

> According to the formula used by Cyprian, the bishop is in the church and the church in the bishop. This affirmation is in accordance with Ignatius, who wrote that where the bishop is, there is the local church. The episcopal ministry cannot be separated from the gifts of the Spirit, which together turn the local church into a place visited by God. And together the local churches form a fellowship of churches.[12]

Tillard deals at length with the role of the synod of the local church or of inter-local churches, attended by the bishop, the presbyterium, the deacons and the laity.[13] He also refers to the expression "particular church" used in the Roman Catholic Church, which is identical with the diocesan local church.[14] The wording of Canon 368 of the Code of Canon Law – "Particular churches in which and from which exists the one and unique Catholic Church are first of all dioceses" – is taken almost literally from the Second Vatican Council's Dogmatic Constitution on the Church *(Lumen Gentium):* "In and from such individual churches there comes into being the one and only Catholic Church" (para. 23).

In affirming this concept of the church built up from below by many individual churches, *Lumen Gentium* cites a reference in a letter of Cyprian to "the one church divided throughout the entire world into many portions". However, the relationship between the individual, particular or local church and the universal church under the primacy of the Roman pontiff was inverted in a Letter of the Congregation for the Doctrine of the Faith, *Communionis Notio* (May 1992), which speaks of an "ontological priority which the universal Church has, in her essential mystery, over every individual particular church".

The 1976 WCC document mentioned earlier, *A Fellowship of Local Churches Truly United,* lists three broad types of local churches:

1. *The local church as the church under the leadership of a bishop*, whose centre is the diocesan see. The bishop, assisted by the presbyterium, presides over the eucharistic assembly. There are several sub-units, parishes, constituted either geographically or on a cultural or linguistic basis. Each is under the care of a presbyter, but all are understood as extensions of the eucharistic assembly of the bishop. This first type is characteristic of the ancient church.

2. *The local church as the church under the leadership of a presbyter.* This view distinguishes between the administrative level of the diocese or region and the liturgical assembly presided over by the presbyter, using the term "local church" only for the latter. This type of local church prevailed in the church of the Middle Ages and is still the common understanding in the Roman Catholic Church. The Lutheran, Reformed and Anglican churches inherited and have largely maintained this position, though in some confessional traditions the emphasis on the celebration of the eucharist has been replaced by an emphasis on the ministry of the word.

3. *The local church as the gathered community.* In this view, characteristic of the Baptist and Congregationalist traditions, the liturgical assembly constitutes its own centre and periphery.

In all traditions, however, a close connection or communion among local churches is considered desirable, even necessary. In early Christianity this communion was established by the mutual recognition of the bishops as representatives of their churches. Beginning in the late Middle Ages and continuing in the Reformation churches, the communion or fellowship of local churches was established by synodal networks. In the Roman Catholic Church diocesan or national synods were celebrated and the bishops gathered in national and regional bishops' conferences. The communion of the bishops with the Roman pontiff is a must for establishing any fellowship or koinonia. In the "congregational" model of local churches, the network of relations is determined by direct community-to-community recognition and fellowship.

This three-part typology of local churches should not be applied too rigidly. As times have changed, so have the churches, including local churches. Pastoral considerations often require different units and sub-units. At the same time, a tendency to establish large units and clusters of local churches can be noted almost everywhere. Yet the present situation should be regarded as an anomaly. The local church has tradition-ally been an example and a sign of church unity; and the existence of several churches in one and the same place, divided along confessional lines, is a denial of the nature and the calling of the local church.

The efforts to reach church unity should primarily aim at enabling all churches in each place to form one local church, regardless of confessional boundaries. Thus dialogues and conversations among the various traditions are needed at all levels, but these should be initiated at the local level. Agreement on the faith and the structure of the church is an essential prerequisite for true unity, a new fellowship, communion or koinonia for the one local church.

A Fellowship of Local Churches Truly United refers to an interesting and challenging new development: the rise of small groups and fellow-ships in many places around common concerns and interests, bringing people together across the barriers of confessional traditions. There are groups to meet the pastoral needs of people living in mixed marriages, groups offering new insights, spiritual experience or liturgical renewal, groups responding to particular problems in society. As they begin to share in worship, in the celebration of the sacraments and in mutual pas-toral ministry, their fellowship acquires an ecclesial quality.

Often the members of these new fellowships accept and remain within their own confessional traditions. But their commitment to the unity of the church leads them to anticipate the communion of the future. These groups are local responses to needs which appear in a particular place. In a certain sense they begin to make real what the local church is called to be. Thus the initiatives of these groups are not entirely local. They reflect the nature of the global church in their determination to centre their life on Jesus Christ and to follow the inspiration and guid-ance of the Holy Spirit.

Such groups present a challenge to the churches which continue to live in separation. The spontaneous experience of unity at the local level is a reminder of the traditional importance of the local church which, together with other local churches, brought about the first fellowship, communion, koinonia and unity of the church of Jesus Christ.

While the local church in its various interpretations is certainly the primary nucleus of the church, the process of internationalization in the world has also had its consequences for the constellation of the churches. The tension within the churches between the local dimension, the terri-torial and national churches, and the growing international dimension has sometimes created serious conflicts – in part because the juridical aspects of this issue have not been adequately recognized or formulated. The updating of church legislation cannot avoid this question. As we shall see in Chapter 7, this matter of the relation between the local and the universal church is equally important for the Roman Catholic Church.

3. Bilateral dialogues

Bilateral religious conversations arose at the time of the Reformation in an effort to avoid permanent divisions in the Western church. Catholics and Lutherans, Lutherans and Anglicans, and Reformed and Lutherans came together to try to find a common denominator to halt the process of division.

In the early 20th century such dialogues resumed between Anglicans and Orthodox and between Lutherans and Reformed – in the search for a common basis. Then, for a time, bilateral dialogues were over-shadowed by multilateral dialogues, supported by the WCC and the Faith and Order Commission. In the 1960s a new emphasis on bilateral dialogues arose; and today a widespread network of both international and national bilateral dialogues, involving nearly all confessional traditions, has become a main element within the modern ecumenical movement.

Two main factors contributed to this development. First, multilateral encounters in the early ecumenical movement, and later within Faith and Order, prepared the ground both theologically and spiritually for more direct meetings between individual churches and confessional denominations. Second, when the Roman Catholic Church became involved in the ecumenical movement after the Second Vatican Council, its outspoken self-understanding, identity and universality stimulated a readiness to engage in bilateral dialogues. Churches with similar characteristics responded positively, without thereby negating or detracting from their bilateral dialogues with other churches.

These bilateral dialogues are officially authorized by the respective church authorities, who appoint the delegates and receive the results. As such, they have a certain authority. They focus primarily on doctrinal matters, and their aim is to overcome the church-dividing divergences inherited from the past and reach agreements that will enable closer fellowship. An undergirding conviction is that the heritage of the past is still alive and must be overcome to establish a lasting fellowship. To avoid the danger that an emphasis on bilateral dialogues can easily lose sight of the overall situation of church divisions, forums on bilateral dialogue have been organized; and it is generally agreed today that both bilateral and multilateral dialogues have their own role to play, and that they fundamentally complement one another.[15]

The churches which take part in bilateral dialogues – about 30 are held on a more or less permanent basis – have different understandings of their dialogue partners and thus of the nature of the dialogue in which they are engaged.

The Orthodox church

For the Orthodox church, the existence of church communities outside the one and undivided Orthodox church does not create ecclesiological problems. Because these communities are perceived as heretical, they situate themselves outside the one true church. At the ecclesiological level, the schism with Rome in the 11th century and the Protestant Reformation of the 16th century did not really touch the Orthodox church: these events just meant an increase in the number of heretical churches. The self-understanding of the Orthodox church as the one and undivided church is a theological and ecclesiological principle; yet in practice the Orthodox have always abstained from exercising missionary activities or establishing a hierarchy in countries with non-Orthodox church governments. The Orthodox church thus seeks to co-exist peacefully with other Christian churches.

The Orthodox are convinced that the present church on earth does not possess the fullness of truth, which remains the distinctive mark of the eschatological church. Orthodox canon law is exclusively related to the earthly existence of the church, during which there is no one who can fulfill the function of primate. Instead, a common body, the ecumenical council, functions as the supreme authority. Because the official canon law comes from the time of the ancient ecumenical councils, it includes no provisions for the present reality of other Christian churches, which are thus positively accepted: the Orthodox church is a full member of the WCC, and it conducts bilateral dialogues with equal partners.[16]

The Roman Catholic Church

We have referred earlier to the statement of *Lumen Gentium* that "the unique Church, constituted and organized in the world as a society, subsists in the Catholic Church which is governed by the successor of Peter and by the bishops in union with that successor". This text from the Second Vatican Council goes on to affirm that outside this unique church of Jesus Christ "many elements of sanctification and of truth can be found. These elements, however, as gifts properly belonging to the church of Christ, possess an inner dynamism towards Catholic unity". The Council's Decree on Ecumenism *(Unitatis Redintegratio)* acknowledges that "both sides" were to blame for the fact that, in the course of the centuries, large communities became separated from full communion with the Catholic Church:

> However, one cannot charge with the sin of the separation those who at present are born into these communities... The Catholic Church accepts them with respect and affection as brothers. For men who believe in Christ and have been properly baptized are put in some, though imperfect, communion with the Catholic Church. Without doubt, the differences that exist in varying degrees between them and the Catholic Church – whether in doctrine and sometimes in discipline, or concerning the structure of the Church – do indeed create many obstacles, sometimes serious ones, to full ecclesiastical communion. The ecumenical movement is striving to overcome these obstacles. But even in spite of them it remains true that all who have been justified by faith in baptism are incorporated into Christ.

The text goes on to affirm that

> very many of the most significant elements and endowments which together go to build up and give life to the Church itself can exist outside the visible boundaries of the Catholic Church: the written Word of God; the life of grace; faith, hope and charity, with the other interior gifts of the Holy Spirit, as well as visible elements. All of these, which come from Christ and lead back to him, belong by right to the one Church of Christ.

Those whom the text calls "our separated brethren" do not have the unity which Jesus Christ wished to bestow on all – that unity which the Holy Scriptures and the revered tradition of the church proclaim.

> For it is through Christ's Catholic Church alone, which is the universal help towards salvation, that the fullness of the means of salvation can be obtained. It was to the apostolic college alone, of which Peter is the head, that we believe that our Lord entrusted all the blessings of the new covenant, in order to establish on earth the one body of Christ into which all those should be fully incorporated who belong in any way to the people of God (para. 3).

It follows from the conviction that the positive elements of sanctification and truth found in non-Catholic churches belong by right to the only church of Christ that the ecumenical movement should undo the defects of the other Christian churches, so that all Christians can be incorporated in the one true church of Jesus Christ, which on earth is identical with the Roman Catholic Church.

Since 1968 the Roman Catholic Church has been officially represented in the WCC Commission on Faith and Order. Twelve Roman Catholic members take an active part in the studies undertaken by the Commission. Notwithstanding these working relationships, the Roman Catholic Church has chosen not to become a WCC member church.

A key question regarding the bilateral dialogues Rome has initiated with various churches is how far these can be considered as genuine dialogues. According to its ecumenical principles, the official Roman Catholic delegations in these dialogues represent the one and unique true church of Jesus Christ. This came clearly to the fore in the Roman Catholic response to the final report of the first Anglican-Roman Catholic International Commission (ARCIC-I) and more recently in the response to the Roman Catholic-Lutheran joint declaration on the doctrine of justification. In each case, the Pontifical Council for Promoting Christian Unity responded to the conclusions of the dialogue after the respective ecumenical partner had done so, formulating these responses in collaboration with the Congregation for the Doctrine of the Faith. Both responses seek or offer a series of further clarifications. Questions are raised about the "authority" of the body which endorses the dialogue. A critical analysis of the responses clearly reveals that the highest Roman authorities are convinced that one partner, the Roman Catholic Church, is the only true church, while the other partner – in these cases the Anglican and Lutheran churches – is defective and possesses only some elements of salvation and truth. The ultimate consequence of the Roman methodology and its underlying conviction is that the goal of the ecumenical movement, the visible unity of the churches, will come about only as restored unity with the Roman Catholic Church.

This self-understanding equally characterizes the 1983 Code of Canon Law. Its practical prescriptions on ecumenism accentuate the existing inequality between the Roman Catholic Church and other Christian churches. What is said about mixed marriages (Canon 1124), the administration of the sacraments of baptism and the eucharist (Canons 844 and 849), the *communicatio in sacris* (Canons 908 and 1365) and the baptism of children of non-Catholic parents (Canons 868 and 1306) attest to this inequality.[17]

The Reformation churches
The churches of the Reformation had to establish that they were identical with the one holy and apostolic church. The right interpretation of the gospel was one indication; the way in which the sacraments were administered was another. The confessions and catechisms underline rather explicitly that the marks of holiness and apostolicity were to apply to their respective churches. On the Lutheran side, for example, Article 7 of the Augsburg Confession defines the church as "the congregation of the holy people, in which the pure doctrine is taught and the sacraments are rightly administered".

Because of their geographical separation in the early Reformation period, each church, whether Lutheran or Reformed, and even each congregation, claimed that it belonged exclusively to the one, holy and apostolic church. The original territorial character of the churches of the Reformation made it even more important to possess these marks of the true church of Jesus Christ, and it is not surprising that in the early years there were doubts about whether churches in other territories displayed these marks. The barriers between Lutherans and Reformed only added to these doubts. The adage *ecclesia semper reformanda*, which implies continuous changes and adaptations to the needs of the times, further complicated the recognition of the marks of the only true church of Jesus Christ.

The acknowledgement of all Protestant churches by the Treaty of Westphalia in 1648 and the subsequent religious and confessional peace inaugurated a process of rapprochement between churches and congregations. The claim of exclusive possession of the marks of the only true church of Jesus Christ diminished in importance. Article 7 of the Augsburg Confession should not be considered as a definition, but rather as a message, Dietrich Bonhoeffer affirmed.[18] Churches and congregations became gradually aware that inter-church relationships do not permit exclusivity but require a supra-confessional attitude.[19] This new ecumenical climate paved the way that led eventually to the Leuenberg Agreement in Europe (1973).

The Anglican Communion

The Anglican church was exclusive in the sense of being set up as a national, established church. Ecclesiologically and doctrinally, however, it has been anything but exclusive: elements of the Reformers' doctrinal views were incorporated into its official teaching, and it is open to all Christian churches. The Anglican church considers itself as a privileged intermediary between the Roman Catholic Church and the Reformation. The conclusion of the final report published by the Anglican-Roman Catholic International Commission (ARCIC-I) in 1982 after 15 years of theological conversations states that the joint commission reached doctrinal agreement on the eucharist, ministry and ordination and authority in the church. "The convergence reflected in our Final Report would appear to call for the establishing of a new relationship between our churches, as a next stage in the journey towards Christian unity."[20] The Final Report was submitted to the authorities of the Roman Catholic Church and the Anglican Communion; and ARCIC-II, convened in 1983, began its work before either side had given a final response to ARCIC-I.

The Lambeth Conference has issued principles and guidelines for relationships with other Christian churches. As a consequence, in recent years a growing number of individual churches have adopted ecumenical laws. The establishment of the Anglican Consultative Council in 1968 was decisive for the ecumenical endeavours of the Anglican communion. One of its aims is promoting the greatest possible Anglican collaboration with the ecumenical movement, particularly with the WCC but also in conversations with the Roman Catholic Church and the Orthodox church.

4. Multilateral dialogues

Most multilateral international ecumenical dialogues have been organized by the WCC through its Commission on Faith and Order. Although both member and non-member churches of the WCC have been involved in these, common ground has been found in the Basis of the WCC. Multilateral dialogues have sometimes benefited from the work of less official movements and meetings of scholars. For example, at the academic level agreements have been reached on exegetical methods and hermeneutical principles, biblical theology, and patristic perspectives on worship and the sacraments. Church participation in these broader conferences and meetings has helped to focus ecumenical reflection on central themes of the Christian faith.

The major church-dividing issues of baptism, eucharist and ministry were already on the agenda at the first Faith and Order world conference (Lausanne 1927). Over the years, Faith and Order gave continued attention to these three issues; and the number of churches participating in this enquiry grew steadily, with active involvement also from non-member churches of the WCC, including the Roman Catholic Church. During an initial stage, an inventory was made of differences in the understanding and practice of baptism, eucharist and ministry, and work was done towards convergence and consensus. A second major goal was mutual recognition by the churches of these three sacraments.

Three texts on baptism, on eucharist and on ministry, drafted on the basis of analytical studies, consultations, discussion in the Faith and Order Commission and responses from churches and other groups, were authorized for distribution by the WCC's fifth assembly (Nairobi 1975). More than a hundred comments were received from churches, theological faculties and other sources, further revisions were made, and at the Faith and Order Commission meeting in Lima, Peru, in 1982, the following motion was unanimously adopted: "The Commission considers the revised text on 'Baptism, Eucharist and Ministry' to have been brought to such a stage of maturity that it is now ready for transmission to the churches." Churches were asked in how far they could "recognize in this text the faith of the church through the ages", "what consequences they could draw from it for their relations, particularly with other churches that also recognize the text as an expression of the apostolic faith", and what guidance they could take from the text for their life and witness.

While the Lima text is not a complete theological treatise on baptism, eucharist and ministry, it does indicate the major areas of theological convergence.[21] The meaning of baptism is explained as "participation in Christ's death and resurrection; conversion, pardoning and cleansing; the gift of the Spirit, incorporation into the Body of Christ; and the sign of the kingdom... Baptism is both God's gift and our human response to that gift" (Baptism, paras 2-8). All churches acknowledge the necessity of faith for the reception of the salvation embodied in baptism. "Both the baptism of believers and the baptism of infants takes place in the church as the community of faith" (para. 12). It is generally agreed that Christian baptism is in water and the Holy Spirit.

The eucharist or Lord's supper is seen as "a gift from the Lord" (Eucharist, para. 1), and every Christian receives the "gift of salvation through communion in the body and blood of Christ" (para. 2). The meaning of the eucharist is explained according to a trinitarian pattern as "thanksgiving to the Father, memorial of Christ, invocation of the Spirit, communion of the Faithful and meal of the kingdom... The church confesses Christ's real, living and active presence in the eucharist", which is "the living and effective sign of his sacrifice, accomplished once and for all on the cross and still operative on behalf of all humankind" (para. 5).

The ordained ministers are located within the general calling of "all members of the church... to confess their faith" (Ministry, para. 4). Their chief responsibility "is to assemble and build up the Body of Christ by proclaiming and teaching the word of God, by celebrating the sacraments, and by guiding the life of the community in its worship, its mission and its caring ministry" (para. 13). The "episcopal succession" is proposed as a "sign, though not a guarantee, of the continuity and unity of the church" (para. 38). "The threefold ministry of bishop, presbyter and deacon may serve today as an expression of the unity we seek and also as a means for achieving it" (para. 22).

An order of worship reflecting the convergences in the Lima text was translated into a great variety of languages and used in many places in eucharistic worship services. The Lima text itself was instrumental in promoting and corroborating inter-church and inter-confessional relationships. Centuries-old boundaries that had prevented churches from familiarizing themselves with one another began to break down as meetings and conferences were organized between churches which never before had been in contact with one another.

The Commission on Faith and Order noted at its meeting in Budapest in 1989 that the more than one thousand written reactions received from all levels and sectors of Christianity worldwide attested to a new ecumenical situation, produced a relevant convergence on fundamental Christian convictions and showed a surprising agreement on concepts which touch the deepest matters of the faith. An important majority had recognized the Lima text as directly related to the apostolic tradition. In this context it had led the churches to reflect critically on the contents of their heritage. It had also been a useful tool in fostering the relationships among the churches, and as such it had become a visible sign of the ecumenical movement on its way towards unity.[22]

5. The juridical consequences of church relationships

The bilateral and multilateral dialogues indicate the desire of churches to create permanent mutual relationships in a world in which the option of isolation is less and less viable.[23] But the growth of inter-church relationships, increasing church networking and "globalization" of the fellowship of churches have juridical consequences.

The point of departure is the sovereignty of the local church as defined above. Every independent local church has the legal right to organize itself, to issue juridical norms and laws and to formulate more permanent matters in its constitution. Both the legislation and the provisions of the constitution are formulated according to the spirit – if not the letter – of the specific confession of faith and the way this confession has been lived out in the different periods of the church's existence. For the most part, this entire complex of legislation, juridical norms and formulations expressing the specific identity of the church and its tradition have almost exclusively served the internal life of the church. Suggestions about participation in the ecumenical movement have recently been inserted into some church constitutions and laws, but the churches' legal frameworks remain largely confined to their internal life.

When churches take up permanent contacts with other churches, agree on collaboration with each other or arrive at doctrinal convergences, they have no legal point of reference at their disposal. Yet the churches do not operate in a legal void. The same church authorities who issue juridical norms for internal church life have the power to come to agreements with other churches. All such external church relations have a juridical dimension. They contribute to building up an inter-church community that has a juridical character. In this way an inter-church, international legal community comes into being.

In formulating the rights and duties that result from collaboration with other churches, as in issuing juridical norms for church law, the identity and confessional self-understanding of a local church remain intact. No harm is done to its sovereignty. Both sets of juridical norms come from a sovereign, independent church with its own rights and duties. Both are intended to serve the proclamation of the word. Every local church has its own juridical power, and so has its partner-church.

The emergence of an ecumenical church law or an ecumenical community with its own specific legislation would not imply that local churches had to renounce their own internal or external legislation or juridical norms and laws. Every church would retain its independence and sovereignty, but the results of its participation in bilateral and multilateral dialogues would create a new reality – a new community of churches related with one another through permanent bonds. Such a new church reality calls for juridical norms. The new international community of churches needs an appropriate legislation that guarantees the independence of each single church but also sets forth the rights and duties that result from inter-church relationships.

6. The legal position of the World Council of Churches

In preparing to mark the 50th anniversary of the WCC in 1998, the Central Committee in 1997 adopted a policy document on the Council's nature and purpose. Based on eight years of study and widespread consultation, this text seeks to set forth a "common understanding and vision" of the specific character of the WCC.[24]

Any discussion of the WCC's self-understanding must begin with the constitutional Basis on which the WCC is founded and with which all member churches express agreement:

> The World Council of Churches is a fellowship of churches which confess the Lord Jesus Christ as God and Saviour according to the Scriptures and therefore seek to fulfill together their common calling, to the glory of the one God, Father, Son and Holy Spirit.

This brief text points to two characteristics which are very important for understanding the specific nature of the WCC. The first is its identification of the WCC as a *fellowship*. It is not itself a church, much less a "super-church". This point was made clearly in a declaration adopted by the Central Committee two years after its founding, at its meeting in Toronto in 1950, which emphasizes in five points what the WCC is *not*, and gives eight positive points which characterize the life of the Council. Second, the Basis emphasizes the *common calling* which the churches seek to fulfil in and through the WCC.

The word "fellowship" is often used to translate the Greek *koinonia*. The theological content of this concept has recently been the subject of much reflection, and it is clear that the relationship among the churches in the WCC is not yet a *koinonia* in the full sense of the word. Fellowship in the sense of *koinonia* is the purpose and aim of the WCC, but it is not yet a reality. Real communion exists among WCC member churches, but this communion is still imperfect. Still, the WCC is more than a functional association of churches set up to organize activities in areas of common interest. The fellowship and the mutual commitment which the churches have established with one another through the WCC are rooted in "the one God, Father, Son and Holy Spirit".

The essence of the WCC is the relationship of the churches with one another, organized and structured to serve as an instrument for the churches as they seek to advance towards *koinonia* in faith, life and witness. The Council should help the churches to seek actively a more perfect communion by promoting stronger relationships. Through this ecumenical commitment the churches open themselves to mutual challenges, including dialogues and binding agreements in the service of deeper and fuller fellowship. The fellowship of the WCC is thus a dynamic, relational reality, embracing the churches as manifestations of the people of God, as communities of faith. Moreover, it is not an end in itself, but exists as a sign and instrument of God's design for humankind.

The emphasis on the member churches' common calling underscores that the WCC is a fellowship of pilgrims on the way towards the same goal, through united action in matters of common interest. This common calling has been put into effect over the past 50 years by facilitating common witness and expressing common concern in the service of human needs.

Membership in the WCC does not affect a church's sovereignty nor change its confessional identity. The churches remain fully free and independent in professing their own theological, ecclesiological, confessional and juridical convictions and in negotiating unions with other churches. The World Council cannot impose any particular concept of the church on its member churches; consequently, membership in the WCC does not oblige a church to consider its own concept of the church as having only relative value. Nor can the WCC impose on member churches the acceptance of a specific doctrine on the nature of church unity.

The member churches of the WCC base their dialogue, cooperation and common witness on the recognition that Christ is the divine Head of the Council and its member churches. The Toronto Statement emphasizes that the member churches should recognize in other churches elements of the true church, consult together regarding the witness the Lord would wish them to bear to the world, express solidarity with one another and enter into spiritual relationships, thus contributing to the renewal of the churches.

A church applying for WCC membership acknowledges its readiness to enter a fellowship of churches and to accept in a permanent and binding way the tasks, obligations and aims of that fellowship. Such a contract between an independent, sovereign church and an already existing fellowship has juridical consequences for both. Both partners have their own ecclesiological and juridical characteristics. The entry of a new member church into the fellowship of churches is a theological, ecclesiological and juridical enrichment for all partners involved, which the WCC has the duty to cultivate and promote.[25]

The member churches within the Council together constitute an international legal community. The Council is not a separate church entity, but is part of a legal community of churches in which both it and the member churches have specific obligations and duties: to advance towards full *koinonia* and visible unity. This legal situation created within the ecumenical movement calls for updating. As noted in Chapter 1, the 1974 Outline already recommended a common effort to allow church legislation to catch up with the ecumenical reality today.

NOTES

[1] Thomas F. Best, ed., *Faith and Renewal,* Geneva, WCC Publications, 1985, pp.194-95.

[2] See Geoffrey Wainwright, "Church", in N. Lossky, et al., eds, *Dictionary of the Ecumenical Movement,* Geneva, WCC Publications, 1991, pp.159-67.

[3] Denzinger, *Enchiridion Symbolorum,* English ed., *The Church Teaches,* p.97.

[4] *Ibid.,* p.75.

[5] Second Vatican Council, Dogmatic Constitution on the Church, *Lumen Gentium,* para. 8. Earlier drafts of the Constitution had used "is", to indicate the total identification of the Roman Catholic Church with the church of Christ; "subsists in" was introduced in the third draft to emphasize elements of the church of Christ in other churches. Subsequently, however, "subsists in" has increasingly been interpreted as an identification of the church of Christ with the Roman Catholic Church.

[6] Colin Buchanan, "Anglican Communion", in *Dictionary of the Ecumenical Movement,* pp.18-20.

[7] On this see Dietrich Pirson, *Universalität und Partikularität der Kirche,* Munich, Claudius Verlag, 1965.

[8] Cited by Gassmann, *Documentary History of Faith and Order, 1963-1993,* p.3.

[9] *Ibid.*

[10] *Ibid.,* pp.3-5.

[11] *Ibid.,* pp.69-75.

[12] J.-M. Tillard, *L'Eglise locale,* pp.219-21.

[13] *Ibid.,* pp.410-50.

[14] *Ibid.,* pp.280ff.

[15] Cf. Harding Meyer, "Bilateral Dialogue", in *Dictionary of the Ecumenical Movement,* pp.280-81; see also, Meyer and L. Vischer, eds, *Growth in Agreement: Reports and Agreed Statements of Ecumenical Conversations on a World Level,* Geneva, WCC Publications, 1984.

16 Dietrich Pirson, *op. cit.,* pp.115-19.

17 If the Roman Catholic Church is the only true church of Jesus Christ, the use of the term "church" for some non-Catholic Christian communities in Council documents and in the Code of Canon Law is ecclesiologically inconsistent. For the churches of the Reformation, the Lutheran and Reformed, the Vatican tends to prefer the term "ecclesial communities".

18 Cf. Dietrich Bonhoeffer, *Gesammelte Schriften,* ed. E. Bethge, Munich, Sanctorum Communio, 1959, Vol. 2, pp.217-18.

19 Dietrich Pirson, *op. cit.,* pp.119-31; Wolfgang Lienemann, "Partikularkirchen und ökumenische Bewegung", in Rau, et al., eds, *Das Recht der Kirche,* Vol. 2, pp.318-70.

20 *The Final Report of the Anglican-Roman Catholic International Commission,* London, CTS/SPCK, 1982.

21 *Baptism, Eucharist and Ministry,* Faith and Order Paper No. 111, Geneva, WCC, 1982; cf. Max Thurian, *"Baptism, Eucharist and Ministry",* in *Dictionary of the Ecumenical Movement,* pp.80-83; *Documentary History of Faith and Order,* pp.24f.

22 *Baptism, Eucharist and Ministry 1982-1990: Report on the Process and Responses,* Geneva, WCC, 1990.

23 Cf. Dietrich Pirson, "Die Ökumenizität des Kirchenrechts", in *Das Recht der Kirche,* Vol. 1, pp.499-517.

24 "Towards a Common Understanding and Vision of the World Council of Churches: A Policy Statement", Geneva, WCC, 1997.

25 For a first effort to delineate the legal position of the WCC, see Dietrich Prison, "Die Rechts-natur des Ökumenischen Rates der Kirchen", in *Universalität und Partikularität der Kirche,* pp.302-24.

CHAPTER 6

The Ecumenical Dialogue on Ethical Issues

The Ten Commandments are generally accepted by all Christians. Roman Catholic and Orthodox canon law include many applications of the commandments to concrete situations. Anglican canon law also refers to them often. Luther and Calvin wrote about the Decalogue as having to be observed by the justified and the elect. According to Calvin, the commandments constitute a guideline for discipline and a source of spirituality. However, except in the Roman Catholic Church there exists no system of their application to concrete cases.

In 1987 the Joint Working Group between the Roman Catholic Church and the WCC began to discuss "new potential and actual sources of divisions within and between the churches". The study came to focus on "personal and social ethical issues and positions as potential sources of discord or common witness".[1] After submitting its first report in 1991, the Joint Working Group was asked to deepen the study not by examining the substance of the potentially or actually divisive issues, but by describing them and outlining

> how they may best be approached in dialogue, in the hope that such issues can offer new opportunities for the increase of mutual understanding and respect and for common witness, without compromise of a church's conviction or of Christian conscience.

1. Personal moral issues: a source of divisions

The Joint Working Group report begins by observing that the contemporary context of cultural and social transformation not only raises questions about traditional moral values and positions but also raises complex new ethical issues. The churches are expected to offer moral guidance, but the guidance they offer is not uniform. The differing church guidelines, particularly with regard to sexual and family ethics, arouse passionate emotions which in turn has negative consequences for ecumenical relationships.

Common ethics for the moral conduct of all Christians would be ideal. Scripture, the common source of all Christian life, does not provide Christians with all the clear moral principles and practical norms they need. The Ten Commandments and the Beatitudes offer only general guidelines. Nevertheless, there is general consensus that through the study of Scriptures and the development of traditions of biblical interpretation, reflection on human experiences and the sharing of insights, Christians can in many cases reach reasonable judgments and decisions on ethical conduct.

In the history of the church, systematic reflection on moral life was developed through the ordering of biblical concepts and images. A distinction was made between first-order principles and second-order rules. The more recent term "hierarchy of values" similarly aims to introduce a certain ordering of ethical ideas.

But Christian traditions and confessional families have different assessments of human nature and the capacity of human reason. Some maintain that sin has so corrupted human nature that reason cannot reach moral truths. Others maintain that sin has only wounded human reason, and that with divine grace reason can reach many truths about moral life. Roman Catholic theology can appeal to a universal divine law through which God orders, directs and governs the whole of creation and humankind. This "natural law" expresses God's will and obliges the human person to seek and know the truth and to live it in conscience. By nature and through grace every person is able to grasp this divine law and discover unchangeable truth.

For the Roman Catholic Church the Magisterium is the authoritative guardian and interpreter of the whole of moral law, both the law of the gospel and natural law. In the Orthodox church decisions on ethical issues rest with the hierarchy, whether an individual bishop or a synod of bishops. Other churches do not ascribe this competence or authority to ministerial leaders. They formulate ethical judgments using various procedures of consultation and decision-making involving both clergy and laity; but no church body has the final authority to define the word of God.

Ecumenical dialogue on moral issues must take account of the nature, mission and structures of the church, the role of ministerial authority, its use of resources in offering moral guidance and the response to the exercise of such authority within the church. Hence it may be asked which practices in various traditions contribute to the legitimate difference and authentic diversity of the moral life of the one church? And how can both common and distinctive practices contribute to the moral richness of the koinonia?

The Joint Working Group report draws the following conclusions:

1. There is agreement that there is a moral universe, grounded in the wisdom and will of God, but different interpretations of God's wisdom exist.

2. Christians share a history of extensive unity in moral teaching and practice, with a shared reflection on the Ten Commandments and the Beatitudes.

3. Some differences among divided Christian communities arise from how they determine and act on moral principles.

4. These differences have led today to such a plurality of moral frameworks and positions within and between the ecclesial traditions that some positions appear to be in sharp tension, even in contradiction. The same constellation of basic moral principles may admit a diversity of rules which intend to express a faithful response to biblical vision and to these principles.

While the report formulates a number of guidelines for common dialogue on ethical issues, these do not eliminate the present divergence and general confusion on ethical issues. Overcoming the divergences will require coming to grips with the real causes of the present confusion and conflicts in the field of ethics.

2. Different theological heritages

Morals and ethics have a fundamentally different place and function in the Roman Catholic Church from that which they have in the churches of the Reformation.[2] In Catholic life morals and ethics have a juridical dimension. Moral theology is closely related to canon law, and the Code of Canon Law includes many prescriptions which strictly pertain to the domain of ethics. Handbooks on moral theology teach Catholics what principles ought to guide their conduct and what actions are morally illicit. While less official than canon law, these manuals do represent the moral teaching based on documents of the magisterium. Likewise, the official *Catechism of the Roman Catholic Church* and the catechisms used in schools contain many elements pertaining to official moral teaching. The manuals used in seminaries treat moral life in all its details, including the degree of seriousness of any transgressions, ranging from venial sins to mortal sins, thus providing priests with material and criteria to evaluate the seriousness of sinful acts and to assign the appropriate penance. Since the priest acts as teacher and judge of morality and the moral laws in his parish, he must know moral law, just as he must be familiar with canon law.

Besides the relationship between the sacrament of penance (oral confession) and the proliferation of ethical and moral literature, a decisive ecclesiological element for the development of Catholic ethical thought is its dependence on the Magisterium, which determines the dogmas and doctrines to be adhered to, the correct interpretation of Scripture and the application of the natural moral law.[3] Sins and infractions of the moral order can thus be determined with precision; and there are catalogues of sins against the Ten Commandments of God and the Five Commandments of the Church. Violations of specific commandments require specific punishments and penances.

Protestant ethics has never had such a "supreme court" to pronounce on what is morally right or wrong. Because Protestant theologians have not been restricted by a superior teaching authority, the history of Protestant ethics shows a much greater diversity. While on many moral matters Protestants have largely accepted the Western individual and collective standards rooted in the Christian tradition, they have not followed the Catholic tradition of referring to Thomas Aquinas. Specific Reformation ethical traditions have retained certain distinctive characteristics, such as the "two realms" in Lutheranism or "church discipline" in Calvinism, but Protestant moral theologians have never been subject to institutional censure.

For Catholic moral thought salvation is always the highest goal. Sins create obstacles to this goal while merits pave the way to it. This is summarized by James Gustafson:

> Western Catholic theology and ethics from the time of Augustine have with remarkable continuity retained a neo-Platonic pattern of all things coming from God and returning to God, *exitus et reditus*. This theological theme embraces and grounds a theological pattern: all things have their proper ends towards which they are oriented by their natures. When humans are properly oriented towards the end for which they have a natural inclination, when they are directed by, and towards, their real good, they are rightly ordered morally and on the right course spiritually. The ultimate end of humans is God; it is contemplation of God, or spiritual communion or friendship with God. Humans are also naturally inclined towards their natural end or good; thus there is a ground for a natural morality available to the knowledge of all rational persons. This ground, theologically interpreted, comes from God; it is graciously given in his creation.[4]

The ultimate end and the natural end are interrelated. Not being oriented towards God causes moral disorder in the personal life and social relationships of the human person. The proper orientation towards the natural good has repercussions on the orientation towards God. An infraction of the natural moral order – that is, sin – has harmful consequences, while right moral acts in accordance with the natural moral order are beneficial for the orientation towards God.

The moral preoccupation to avoid sin – on the one hand discerning sin in one's relationships with other persons and in almost all human activities, on the other hand enjoying the security that through the sacrament of penance friendship with God is restored – has profoundly influenced Catholic life-style over the centuries. In the last generation, however, this life-style has rapidly been losing importance. One factor in this development is far more familiar relationships between Catholics and Protestants.

From the outset, the Catholic preoccupation with avoiding sin for the sake of salvation sounded to the Reformers like "works-righteousness", as if salvation were earned through meritorious works rather than received as a free gift of God's grace. For the Reformers existential human sinfulness was far more basic than immoral acts. Particular sins are the fruit of fundamental sinfulness. The essential issue is not whether a human person is oriented towards God, but whether he or she trusts or mistrusts God. Philip Melanchthon explained the difference in the understanding of sin between the followers of Luther and the "scholastics" (Catholics) as follows:

> When the scholastics talk about original sin, they do not mention the more serious faults of human nature, namely ignoring God, despising him, lacking fear and trust in him, hating his judgment and fleeing it, being angry at him, despairing his grace, trusting in temporal things, etc. These evils, which are most contrary to the law of God, the scholastics do not even mention. We wanted to show that original sin also involves such faults as ignorance of God, contempt of God, lack of the fear of God and of trust in him, inability to love him. These are the chief imperfections in human nature, transgressing as they do the first table of the Decalogue.[5]

It is noteworthy that the emphasis here is no longer on the fundamental orientation towards the ultimate goal, God, but on trust or mistrust, respect or contempt for him. This change of emphasis is significant for the relation between morality and salvation. "If original sin and sins as such are fundamentally a violation of the 'first table of the Decalogue', it is basically a religious problem rather than a moral problem... If sin is basically a religious problem, its answer has to be basically a religious answer, not a moral answer."[6] Faith has to be a response to a free gift of God's grace. And God's grace was seen first and foremost as mercy with regard to the fundamentally sinful human being. In this sense, rigorous adherence to norms and rules of right moral conduct is a peripheral issue for the Reformation.

For Protestantism sins do not have to be counted and classified. They are included in the root cause of sin, the violation of the first commandment of the Decalogue, which does not allow any reliance on moral righteousness. Hence, moral theology and ethics receive an essentially different dimension. If salvation, the core of the Christian religion, is reached through God's gratuitous grace, then moral life, though serious and important, is embedded in a different religious and theological context.

For Calvin, original sin had one root – the sinfulness and corruption of human nature:

> Original sin... seems to be a hereditary depravity and corruption of our nature, diffused into all parts of the soul, which first makes us liable to God's wrath, then also brings forth in us those works which Scripture calls "works of the flesh" [Gal. 5:19]. And that is properly what Paul often calls sin. The works that come forth from it – such as adulteries, fornications, thefts, hatreds, murders, carousings – he accordingly calls "fruits of sin" [Gal. 5:19-21], although they are commonly called "sins" in Scripture, and even by Paul himself.
>
> We must, therefore, distinctly note these two things. First, we are so vitiated and perverted in every part of our nature that by this great corruption we stand justly condemned and convicted before God, to whom nothing is acceptable but righteousness, innocence and purity... Even infants themselves... are guilty not of another's fault but of their own... Indeed, their whole nature is a seed of sin; hence it can be only hateful and abhorrent to God. From this it follows that it is rightly considered sin in God's sight, for without guilt there would be no accusation...
>
> Then comes the second consideration: that this perversity never ceases in us, but continually bears new fruits – the works of the flesh that we have already described – just as a burning furnace gives forth flame and sparks, or water ceaselessly bubbles from a spring.[7]

The first element in the salvation of the human being for Calvin as for Luther is the gracious gift of righteousness offered by God. The consequences of corruption and depravity, sins, haunt the human being all through life. No one can earn salvation on the basis of moral merits. On the other hand, Calvin does insist on sanctification, on obedience to God's law:

> [The Spirit] has been given to us for sanctification in order that he may bring us, purged of uncleanness and defilement, into obedience to God's righteousness. This obedience cannot stand except when the inordinate desires to which these men would slacken the reins have been tamed and subjugated.[8]

In his discussion Calvin stresses continuity between the natural moral law, the Decalogue and the moral teachings of Jesus. As Gustafson notes,

> In this respect there are significant similarities to the ethics of the Catholic tradition. But [Calvin] also shared Luther's conviction that grace – both forgiv-

ing and sanctifying – is a gift, and not earned. Since he was concerned with how the Christian life ought to be lived, for him the principal use of the law was the so-called "third use".[9]

There are also convergences between Catholic and Protestant ethics and morality – for example, regarding the natural law, which according to the Reformers is engraved on all human hearts. For Calvin, "whatever God requires of us (because he can require only what is right), we must obey out of natural obligation".[10] Biblically based ethics can be ethics for all, since its ultimate moral reference point is "written, even engraved, upon the hearts of all".

Melanchthon expresses a similar view:

> The third and principal use, which pertains more closely to the proper purpose of law, finds its place among believers in whose hearts the Spirit of God already lives and reigns. For even though they have the law written and engraved upon their hearts by the finger of God, that is, have been so moved and quickened through the directing of the Spirit that they long to obey God, they still profit by the law in two ways... It is the best instrument for them to learn more thoroughly each day the nature of God's will... The servant of God will also avail himself of this benefit of the law; by frequent meditation upon it to be aroused to obedience, be strengthened in it, and be drawn back from the slippery path of transgression.[11]

The report of the Joint Working Group mentioned above affirms that "Christians enjoy a history of substantial unity in moral teaching and practice. By placing ethical issues within this inheritance of moral unity, we can more carefully understand the origin and nature of any present disagreement or division." Divergent or convergent teachings on particular moral issues arise out of different heritages in which there are varying emphases and assessments. Clearly the different moral teachings and ethical principles are not isolated; and history has shown that any theological or ethical problem must not be addressed separately from the more fundamental questions. As one of the "Guidelines for Ecumenical Dialogue on Moral Issues" which conclude the report states:

> When the dialogue continues to reveal sincere but apparently irreconcilable moral positions, we affirm in faith that the fact of our belonging in Christ is more fundamental than the fact of our moral differences. The deep desire to find an honest and faithful resolution of our disagreements is itself evidence that God continues to grace the koinonia among disciples of Christ.

3. Divergences in social and political ethics

The ecumenical movement has always considered social and political responsibility at the international level a major task for the churches.

Here too there is no uniformity in the Christian world. Roman Catholic theologian Charles E. Curran observes:

> The topic of the church and morality involves not only the internal moral life of the church, but also the role of the church in the moral life of society and the nation. All recognize the manifold moral problems facing our world today. The Christian gospel calls for Christians as the community of the disciples of Jesus to work for a more free, just and peaceful world. But great divisions exist within and among the churches on many of these issues. Here too the question acutely arises about unity and diversity within the individual church and among the churches. Where should there be unity, and where should there be diversity?[12]

The complexity of the modern world – changes in the means of production and political reactions to these, new cultural trends, ideological struggles, liberation and emancipation movements – has raised many questions whose significance the confessional churches have often discerned only very slowly and to which their traditional theological and ethical concepts have no ready-made answers.

In developing their social and political ethics in response to a rapidly changing world, the churches have tried to be faithful to their traditional confessional convictions. However, with the founding and growth of the WCC, a new constellation developed: on the one side were the Protestants, including the Anglicans, and later the Orthodox; on the other side the Roman Catholics. These two groups not only have distinct methods for guiding the faithful with regard to individual or personal ethics but also diverge on social and political ethics. The Joint Working Group commissioned a study by Thomas Sieger Derr, published in 1983, to spell out why cooperation between the WCC and the Roman Catholic Church did not function well with regard to social and political questions. He writes:

> The methodological difference most often mentioned is the Roman Catholic preference for relating positions on social questions to the tradition of natural law ethics, and the World Council's predilection for discovering the divine revelation in the freshness and uniqueness of each event.[13]

WCC statements on social or political matters are a response to a particular situation or even to a general principle, in which the assessment of the principle is clearly influenced by the particular characteristics of the situation or event. This has given rise in Roman Catholic circles to the opinion that although World Council statements may be cloaked in the guise of religious ethics, they in fact belong more to the political order than to the moral order. Thus, the general idea is that politics take precedence over theology, to the extent that instead of sacred and religious judgments Geneva produces secular statements.

In the 1970s, the WCC often spoke of an "action-reflection" model for Christian social ethics, describing this integration of study and action as typically biblical, with theology emerging not systematically but as a reflection on concrete situations. For example, M.M. Thomas, moderator of the WCC Central Committee, said at the Nairobi assembly (1975): "I welcome the intercontextual method of theologizing which has come into being in Faith and Order, and the action-reflection method which has come to dominate the WCC's programmes of justice and service."[14]

Documents issued by the Vatican demonstrate a higher level of abstraction, in conformity with Roman Catholic tradition, dealing more with general principles than with particular situations or events. Specific situations may be the occasion for statements, but even so these start from general principles developed in the tradition of Catholic thinking and are formulated systematically in such a way as to be applicable to all similar situations in the past, present and future. The Catholic tradition is marked by natural law. The biblical references that inspire Christian ethics are integrated in the long tradition rather than heard afresh in a contemporary context. The Vatican states the principle in theory, avoiding condemnation of any authority, social class or person, and leaving the application to others. It should be noted that the Roman Catholic magisterium claims competence to interpret the natural moral law, illuminated and enriched by divine revelation.

A decisive methodological or procedural divergence is also evident in the approach to and judgment of ideologies. The WCC has listened to revolutionary ideologies and sympathized with Christians who found in Marxism a powerful tool in the defence of the poor and oppressed. The church should not necessarily take sides ideologically, but it must recognize the positive use of ideologies for justice, particularly when they are consonant with Christian values. By contrast,

> official Vatican documents have sharply condemned Marxist theology. It is condemned for its atheistic materialism, its dialectic of violence, the way it absorbs individual freedom in the collectivity, at the same time denying all transcendence to man, for its doctrine of class war, and for its oppression of religion. It is wrong to think we can accept Marxism on one level and reject it on others, for all are bound together and end in a totalitarian and violent society.[15]

Other revolutionary and liberal ideologies have also been condemned by Rome. Their contents have been criticized, and the general conviction that Catholic social and political teachings should remain independent of any secular ideology has been maintained, on the ground that the kingdom of God will be reached through faith and perfect moral behaviour, not through human commitment to the improvement of the world or political, economic and social liberation. The Roman Catholic Church has a religious mission, not a worldly one, as Pope John Paul II has often emphasized. The WCC on the other hand has seen it as a Christian obligation to be involved in the struggle for political, social and economic liberation. Such a commitment on the part of Christians is a manifestation of the presence of the kingdom already here and now.

There is also a difference in the approach taken to public cases of injustice and human rights violations. The Vatican prefers to change people's behaviour and attitudes through quiet diplomacy, avoiding public condemnation of individuals and peoples. This method is in itself conservative, intending to disturb the *status quo* as little as possible. The WCC is much less concerned with the established order. It is not a church but a movement that intends to make known its standpoint. Its condemnations and denunciations are made available to the press. It wants to take up the role of the prophets of the past.

These differences can be related to the structural differences between a world church and a council of non-Catholic churches. The Vatican is the central office of a single worldwide church with an ecclesiology of its own. This emphasizes its unity. With its unique position as the true church, it governs authoritatively and proclaims what all its members must accept or refuse. The WCC as a council of non-Catholic churches has only moral and not ecclesiological authority. It does not speak for its members and acts on their behalf only in matters which they specifically entrust to it. The members are not bound to accept its assessments or judgments and may indeed dissociate themselves from them. The authority of what WCC assemblies and Central Committees say and do lies only in the weight of its own truth and wisdom. Nevertheless, as we have noted, the development of ecumenical relationships has created a new configuration between the WCC and its member churches which does have juridical implications, also at the level of practical decisions to be taken by member churches.

In the Roman Catholic tradition, human rights are based on the natural law and can be discovered by human reason. The natural law reflects the mind of God in created things and is confirmed in revelation. The WCC's attitude towards human rights is inspired by a variety of traditions. The Anglo-Saxon tradition stresses individualism, which is derived from the natural law tradition. The European Reformation emphasized the primacy of a community of mutual service. In practice, both the Holy See and the WCC ground human rights in the inherent dignity of the human person and thus echo the concepts and terminology of the Universal Declaration of Human Rights (1948). Both expand human rights from individuals to classes, groups and peoples, and consider misery, poverty and political oppression as violations of basic rights.

On the question of religious liberty both the WCC and the Vatican support Article 18 of the Universal Declaration of Human Rights: "Everyone has the right to freedom of thought, conscience and religion: this right includes... freedom, either alone or in community with others and in public or private, to manifest his religion or belief in teaching, practice, worship and observance." Both have often emphasized that the freedom of communities to profess and practise their religion is an essential element for peaceful human co-existence and for peace in the world.

The WCC Central Committee in 1980 endorsed the commitment of churches and Christians who "in several societies, with different political systems and social backgrounds that grossly violate basic human rights, have become actively involved in struggles for justice and human rights, based on their sincere understanding of the gospel of Christ".

Similarly, the WCC and the Vatican hold the same strong theoretical position regarding racism. Racism is an unutterable offence against God, to be endured no longer, according to the Council, an inadmissible affront to the fundamental rights of the human person, in the words of Rome. But divergences arise as soon as these statements are applied to particular situations. The WCC names persons and lists situations of racial discrimination in various nations. It concentrates its attack on white racism, and it does not spare the churches. The Vatican is bound to formulate its statements in more general terms. Diplomatic relationships with governments forbid public condemnations.

War is a subject of perennial controversy in Christian ethics:

> While pacifism is the most ancient tradition in the church, it is not the dominant one in either the WCC or the Roman Catholic Church. There are important pacifist elements in both fellowships and both speak seriously of peace education. But both acknowledge in practice the tradition of "just war" – a concept that originated in the ancient world, and was eventually brought into the church and developed there.[16]

But the production, deployment and threats to use nuclear weapons for mass destruction have so underminded the credibility of the just war theory that more and more Christians are concluding that a just war is no longer possible. The 1979 NATO decision to deploy a new generation of cruise and Pershing nuclear missiles in Europe to counter the threat of the Soviet SS-20s provoked protest and resistance among the populations concerned. In many countries Christians took the lead against nuclear deterrence and promoted the organization of nonviolent movements.[17] A 1981 public hearing on nuclear weapons organized by the WCC concluded that nuclear weapons as such are evil and that the possession and the readiness to use them are wrong in the sight of God:

> We believe that the time has come when the churches must unequivocally declare that the production and deployment as well as the use of nuclear weapons are a crime against humanity and that such activities must be condemned on ethical and theological grounds.

The WCC assembly in Vancouver (1983) endorsed these conclusions.

The Vatican assessment of nuclear deterrence was different. In an authoritative address to the 1983 special session on disarmament of the United Nations General Assembly, the Vatican representative said: "In current conditions deterrence based on balance, certainly not as an end in itself, but as a step on the way towards a progressive disarmament, may still be judged morally acceptable."[18]

4. Social and political ethics in the ecumenical movement

The well-known conference of the Life and Work movement on "Church, Community and State" (Oxford 1937) underscored that Christian ethical and moral concern cannot be limited to the commitments of individual Christians alone, but must engage the churches as well. In the years to come, the centrality of the Lordship of Christ became a dominant theme in the ecumenical approach to social and political ethics. The struggle of the Confessing Church in Germany with National Socialism provoked questions about what kind of conduct Christians could envisage with respect to the state, the economy and political situations, given that these are intimately related with natural and positive law.

In the early history of the WCC, the relationship of law and justice to the authority of the Bible was the object of intense study and reflection.[19] Several conferences debated questions of natural law, law and ethics, and international law, as well as the question of the trinitarian and Christological approach to law and justice. These culminated in a conference in Treysa, Germany, in 1950. Roger Mehl summarizes the ecumenical insights as follows:

- Resisting the opposing dangers of anarchy and tyranny, Christians and churches must defend the constitutional state, in which all citizens enjoy equality before the law and are judged according to their actions measured against a law promulgated before these actions.
- Christians and churches must point out and denounce violations of justice and strive for as close as possible a conformity of law to justice. Revolution may be necessary as a last resort in a situation of flagrant injustice.

– Christians and churches should constantly re-examine the law established by legislators, not only because it may be unjust but because it may *become* unjust as a result of new realities or developments in science. While recognizing the need for legislation, conscience and responsibility may in certain circumstances set a limit to the intervention of law.

– Christians and churches regard the word of God as the norm for their conduct and this norm holds good whenever a body of law has to be formulated and promulgated with authority. But Scripture neither provides ready-made answers to all legal problems nor makes it possible to formulate "Christian legislation". Scripture provides indications, directions and warnings about limits that may not be transgressed. The life and teaching of Jesus Christ offer the fundamental inspiration of the law of love.

– The law authorizes, forbids and punishes. In making law, Christians and churches should do their utmost to ensure that the law remains analogous to the order and justice of the kingdom of God. The making of law is an ethical task which cannot be left to political authorities and experts alone. Christians and churches should watch the making of law and its execution, reminding themselves that as followers of Jesus Christ they have a responsibility in the preparation of God's kingdom.[20]

From the beginning the WCC has sought a vision of society that could give concrete guidance for Christian ethical conduct in the political and social setting arising from the legislation in force.

> When the ecumenical discussion on social thought resumed after the second world war... Europe was in ruins, vividly illustrating the human disorder identified in the theme of the Amsterdam assembly. Colonial empires were breaking down, and the years to come would see the independence of former Asian and African colonies... States and churches had to adapt to a situation in which most of the previous paradigms of social and political thought had to be re-evaluated and most of the discussions of social and ethical concerns would be influenced by the ideological undercurrent and hostilities emanating from the East-West confrontation.[21]

As early as the Amsterdam assembly, the concept of the "responsible society" had emerged. With laissez-faire capitalism and totalitarian communism both making promises they could not fulfil, the assembly called on Christians "to seek new, creative solutions which never allow either justice or freedom to destroy the other". No civilization can escape the radical judgment of the word; thus none is to be accepted uncritically. The assembly affirmed furthermore that war is contrary to the will of God, that every kind of tyranny and imperialism should be opposed, and that efforts to ensure all people basic human liberties, especially religious freedom, should be defended and promoted. In the wake of the Amsterdam assembly the WCC initiated studies on "The Responsible Society", "Moral Problems in Economic and Political Life" and "Moral Problems in the Economic Situation Today".

The second WCC assembly (Evanston 1954) related the understanding of the responsible society to contemporary social problems, especially in the developing regions. Evanston reaffirmed the responsibility of churches and Christians for peace and justice, and urged governments to ban all weapons of mass destruction.

The New Delhi assembly in 1961 discussed ethical problems in politics, economics and society in the light of rapid changes in the third world. The assembly took a renewed stand on religious liberty and adopted a resolution on anti-semitism. The WCC assumed increased responsibility for relief to people in distress, refugees and victims of catastrophes.

To a great extent, the fourth assembly (Uppsala 1968) followed the findings of the World Conference on Church and Society held in Geneva in 1966. The assembly did not abandon the theological understanding of the church's ethical function in society as formulated by earlier assemblies, but offered justification for revolution against the established order, arguing that overt revolutionary violence may sometimes be a lesser evil than the covert violence of authorities who condemn entire populations to perennial despair. The reality that the rich were becoming richer and the poor were becoming poorer dominated the socio-political and economic discussions. Uppsala also debated how churches and Christians make right ethical decisions.

> Social and cultural differences make a single style of Christian life impossible. Refusing to choose between "contextualism" and "rules", the assembly pressed for the position that individual moral choices can be made only in a Christian community which is held together by biblical insight and the communion table.[22]

It was in the wake of the Uppsala assembly that the WCC initiated its Programme to Combat Racism.

The fifth assembly (Nairobi 1975) introduced the search for a "Just, Participatory and Sustainable Society", which was considered to be more adequate than the earlier idea of a "responsible society". In 1977 an advisory committee for this new programme thrust was appointed. Rather than trying to elaborate the blueprint for a Christian model of an ideal society, it carried out its search, which included an intensive build-up of regional networks, in the context of the contemporary reality of people's struggles for justice, participation and sustainability. Two years later, a study on political ethics began with the examination of power structures, participation and political organization on the local, national and international levels. Within this context should be located "contextual liberation ecumenism" and the participatory Christian social ethics of the WCC, based on an overriding concern for the rights of the poor and the oppressed, and the need to be in solidarity with them.[23]

The sixth assembly (Vancouver 1983) recommended that the WCC give priority to engaging its member churches "in a conciliar process of mutual commitment to Justice, Peace and the Integrity of Creation", whose foundations were "confessing Christ as the life of the world and Christian resistance to the demonic powers of death in racism, sexism, caste oppression, economic exploitation, militarism, violations of human rights and the misuse of science and technology".[24]

In 1991, the Canberra assembly confirmed this direction:

> Social justice cannot happen apart from a healthy environment, and a sustainable and sustaining environment will not come about without greater social justice... The biblical concept of justice recognizes the need for healthy relationships in creation as a whole. This way of viewing justice helps to understand the linkage between poverty, powerlessness, social conflict and environmental degradation.[25]

The Canberra assembly strongly endorsed the Ecumenical Decade of Churches in Solidarity with Women, inaugurated in 1988, which focused on empowering women at all levels to participate more fully in decision-making that affects their destiny, to be partners with men in shaping the lives of their families and their societies, and to be equipped for ministry in the churches in the full fellowship of the people of God.

NOTES

[1] "The Ecumenical Dialogue on Moral Issues, Potential Sources of Common Witness or of Divisions", in *Joint Working Group between the Roman Catholic Church and the World Council of Churches: Seventh Report*, Geneva, WCC Publications, 1998, pp.31-42.

[2] James M. Gustafson, *Protestant and Roman Catholic Ethics: Prospects for Rapprochement*, Chicago, Univ. of Chicago Press, 1978.

[3] Pope Leo XIII in his letter on *Human Liberty* (1888) referred to "the Church, the pillar and ground of truth, and the unerring teacher of morals".

[4] Gustafson, *op. cit.*, p.7.

[5] Philip Melanchthon, *Apology of the Augsburg Confession*, Art. 2 (Original Sin), in Theodore G. Tappert, ed., *The Book of Concord*, Philadelphia, Muhlenberg Press, 1959, pp.101f.

[6] Gustafson, *op. cit.*, p.9.

[7] John Calvin, *Institutes of the Christian Religion*, II.1.8.

[8] *Ibid.*, III.3.14.

[9] Gustafson, *op. cit.*, p.18.

[10] *Institutes*, II.7.2.

11 Cf. Clyde L. Manschreck, *Melanchthon on Christian Doctrine*, New York, Oxford U.P., 1965, pp.122-28.

12 Charles E. Curran, *The Church and Morality: An Ecumenical and Catholic Approach,* Minneapolis, Fortress Press, 1993, p.10.

13 Thomas Sieger Derr, *Barriers to Ecumenism: The Holy See and the World Council of Churches on Social Questions*, Maryknoll NY, Orbis, 1983. Much of what follows is based on his research, since he had access to authoritative sources from the two partners.

14 David Paton, ed., *Breaking Barriers: Official Report of the Fifth Assembly of the WCC,* Geneva, WCC Publications, 1976, p.237.

15 Derr, *op. cit.,* p.52.

16 *Ibid.*

17 Cf. Marc Reuver and Friedhelm Solms, *Churches as Peacemakers?,* Rome, IDOC, 1985; and Marc Reuver, *Christians as Peacemakers: Peace Movements in Europe and the USA*, Geneva, WCC Publications, 1988.

18 Cited by Reuver, *Christians as Peacemakers,* p.40.

19 José Miguez Bonino, "Ethics", in Lossky, et al., *Dictionary of the Ecumenical Movement,* pp.364-69.

20 Roger Mehl, "Law", in *ibid.*, pp.509f.

21 Ans van der Bent, *Commitment to God's World: A Concise Critical Survey of Ecumenical Social Thought*, Geneva, WCC Publications, 1995, p.23.

22 Ans van der Bent, "WCC Assemblies", in *Dictionary of the Ecumenical Movement,* pp.1090-96.

23 Ans van der Bent, *Commitment to God's World,* pp.49f.

24 David Gill, ed., *Gathered for Life: Official Report of the Sixth Assembly of the WCC,* Geneva, WCC Publications, 1983, pp.131f.

25 Michael Kinnamon, ed., *Signs of the Spirit: Official Report of the Seventh Assembly of the WCC,* Geneva, WCC Publications, 1991, p.55.

CHAPTER 7

Church Law in Modern Society

The Faith and Order Outline of 1974 (see Chapter 1) which called for the adjustment of church law to the new ecumenical realities noted that all Christian churches and communities have a concrete legal form. All have their own inner structure and occupy a social and legal space acknowledged by society.

Each of the various legal forms which regulate the life of Christian churches and confessions stems from a specific understanding of the gospel. As we have seen in the earlier chapters, the characteristics and differences which mark the legal systems of the confessional families have their origins in history and are influenced by the confessions of faith.

Today as in the past church legislations are marked by the specific political and civil setting, the larger society of which the churches are a part, with which they are in permanent contact and in which they exercise their mission. The different specific church-state relationships have been determinative for church legislations. The development of both churches and states has provoked a certain tendency towards uniformity, which has blunted the sharpest differences, and resulted in mutual approaches and relationships. It is well known that this tendency on the global level faces opposite currents. Fortunately these affect the life of the churches only indirectly.

1. Characteristics of modern church legislation

Since the end of the second world war and the founding of the World Council of Churches in 1948, Christian churches and communities have been strongly influenced by the networks created by the ecumenical movement. The traditionally isolated life of the churches has increasingly given way to a new style of working together and taking common initiatives and decisions, with Christian unity as the ultimate goal.

The Outline of 1974 emphasizes that ecumenical commitment and the resulting new relations have fundamentally influenced the juridical life of the churches. However, only rarely and hesitantly have church legislations, their legal form and their systems of law been adapted to the changed realities, and no uniform juridical pattern for this has emerged. According to the Outline these adjustments should be shaped in conformity with the norms and rules of church legislation in force. The reality of new permanent relationships, agreements and unions between churches and church communities has not been translated into adequate juridical terms and legal forms. Thus no legal foundation exists for current ecumenical initiatives, projects, programmes and unions.

Only after the second world war did church law become an independent academic discipline in the churches of the Reformation, related to theology, and to civil, public and international law.[1] The Barmen Synod gave a strong impulse to the development of Protestant church law as a science. While a few monographs had been written on various issues, church law now became an autonomous study, of which Erik Wolff, Johannes Heckel, Karl Barth and Hans Dombois were the pioneers. Since these early years, the relationship between church law and civil law, as well as the particular features of the existing church legislation, have become part of university curricula and specialized seminars. The writings of Luther and Calvin have been re-read for their specific thoughts on canon law, and the traditional Lutheran and Reformed heritage in the field of church law has been re-interpreted and applied to modern times.

This new science understands church legislation as qualitatively different from other juridical systems in force in modern societies. Church law is unique because it is fundamentally Christocentric, in conformity with Scriptures. The specific character of church law is clear in its *ius liturgicum*, in prescriptions concerning church life and in the relationship between law and faith. The *ius liturgicum* includes the legitimation of the proclamation of the word of God and the administration of the sacraments. However, church law and civil or state law also have many subjects and features in common.

Although churches and church communities are part of a nation or a state, theologically speaking their law system can be neither neutral nor unrelated to a confession of faith. This has become particularly evident in the experience of churches under dictatorial political regimes. The Barmen Synod (1934) offers clear proof of why church law is to be independent and a legitimate and justified instrument of church government. According to the text issued by the Barmen Synod, the role of church law is fundamentally one of witness. There is an unbreakable link between the mission of the church and its legislation, between faith and obedience. While many issues are of course common concerns of both state and church, the text of the Barmen Synod emphasizes that church legislation should have its own nature, especially with regard to its own institutional structure.

Three distinct levels are generally identified in explaining the relationship between church laws and state laws in modern democratic nations. First, on the political level of the state there is a category of church laws which are directly associated with official state norms and juridical prescriptions. The second level comprises domains which are the common concern of both state and church; at this level church laws should respect state ordinances, whether national, territorial or local. The third level is the specific legislation regulating the internal life of the church; this includes laws regarding the proclamation of the word, worship, the administration of the sacraments, church membership and its eventual termination, and the government and officials of the church.

The Roman Catholic Church has a system of concordats for dealing with its relations to states. It is "the task of the pontifical delegate to deal with questions concerning the relations between the church and the state, and in a specific manner to deal with the drafting and implementation of concordats and other agreements of this type" (Canon 365).

Protestant church lawyers, following the teaching of the Reformers, argue that church legislation and individual church laws are not directly related to divine law and consequently are not to be considered means of salvation. They were made by human persons, although they should be rooted in Scripture and therefore belong explicitly to the domain of theology. Consequently, church legislation is not considered to be constitutive of the nature of the church, but consecutive, and as such a result of the historical development of the specific character of each church.

Most Protestant church lawyers recognize the three distinct levels of church laws mentioned above, though some distinguish only two categories – those regulating the internal affairs of the church and those concerned with its relations with the outside world. Rarely has the category of church laws resulting from ecumenical dialogues, agreements and unions between churches and Christian communities been taken into account.

The traditional Protestant concern with the dialectic of justice and love, law and grace, is reflected in the debate over whether church law should include sanctions. The gospel does not blot out the law. The tension between the two is a feature of the earthly existence of the faith. The church as a community of faith sharing in this earthly existence must live with this tension; and this is reflected in the "earthliness" of church law and its theological dimension. Church legislation represents positive human law; it is the task of theology to underline the relationships of these laws with Scripture, confessions of faith and witness. Fundamentally, church legislation aims at communicating the word of God.

Recent studies of church law have taken up anew the concept of *ius divinum*. Here Roman Catholic and Protestant understandings differ markedly. The Code of Canon Law, as we have seen, continues the tradition initiated by Gratian in the 12th century. Canon 24 asserts that "no custom which is contrary to divine law, whether natural or positive law, can obtain the force of law." According to the present Code, the institutions *de iure divino* are the hierarchy, which has the faculty of ordination and jurisdiction, the primacy of the pope and the sacraments. Positive juridical norms are very rarely founded on *ius divinum,* but it is considered to be the fundamental source of infallible pronouncements in doctrine and morals. The Reformers and their followers do not accept the Catholic interpretation of either *ius divinum* or the role of canon law. Some Protestant circles have understood the concept to mean being in accordance "with God's word".

In recent times the importance of the appeal to *ius divinum* seems to have diminished. On the one hand, secularization has undermined the influence of natural law; on the other hand, increasing criticism of the identification of *mandatum Christi* with the gospel and Scripture has led also to questioning of the concept of *ius divinum* in church legislation.

Besides the question of whether the concept of *ius divinum* can be traced back to the apostolic church is the issue of whether the idea of divine right can be translated into juridical terms – for if it cannot be, then *ius divinum* is not the nucleus of church legislation, nor does church legislation contain irreversible contents. The prevailing Protestant interpretation relates *ius divinum* not to church law systems, but rather to the permanent activity of the Spirit in the church and to the presence of Christ in the life of the church. In this sense, the question of *ius divinum* becomes a theological issue regarding the foundation of the church and its fundamental characteristics – the proclamation of the word and the administration of the sacraments of baptism and the Lord's supper.

Since the church is a community of believers who are sinners, the prescriptions of church legislation maintaining the necessary order include measures of constraint and penal disciplinary sanctions. A community of believers which has legislative power should also have the faculty of issuing penal laws and covering members who offend them. Here two differences appear between Protestant and Roman Catholic understandings.

The Roman Catholic Church considers itself a *societas perfecta,* with its own and independent system of penal laws. The Code of Canon Law stipulates: "The church has an innate and proper right to coerce offending members of the Christian faithful by means of penal sanctions" (Canon 1311). Those who violate church laws can be deprived of certain rights and authority, such as the right to attend worship and receive the sacraments. Canon 1329 enumerates automatic penalties (*latae sententiae*) and inflicted penalties (*ferendae sententiae*); further distinctions are made among different penalties: expiatory penalties, suspensions (for members of the clergy), penal remedies, excommunication. The Code also provides a whole system of tribunals and trials. Every member of the Roman Catholic Church can be judged except the bishop of Rome, who, as pope and primate, is not accountable to any authority (Canon 1404).

From the beginning, the Reformation emphasized right order within the local congregation and the discipline of its members. The Lutheran and Reformed churches from the outset inflicted penal sanctions, including excommunication, on members who seriously disturbed or violated order within the congregation or acted against the common good of the members. Over time, the Protestant churches were also obliged to accommodate their church legislation to changing needs. The real emancipation of civil authorities and especially of territorial governers marked for many churches the beginning of their own church law systems.

Law, correction and punishment have been permanently controversial subjects in Protestant churches. How is the relation between penal law and the commandment of love to be understood? While the realm of law is not that of love, the fundamental aim of law is to promote justice, in view of love. Within the church as a visible assembly of sinning believers, the law authorizes, forbids and punishes. In creating laws, Christian churches should attempt to ensure that, despite their inadequacies, these laws defend order and justice in view of the commandment of love. Law is not ethics, but creating and formulating laws, including penal laws, are ethical acts, which cannot be entrusted to political authorities alone nor left in the hands of experts who are not Christians and are not familiar with Christian life.

In the Protestant tradition, the church is both the invisible assembly of believers and an empirical reality. Ecclesiology studies both aspects of the church and the tension between them. Some Protestant ecclesiological studies interpret the Reformers' distinction between the invisible "spiritual" church and the visible "juridical" church to imply an extreme separation, even contradiction, between Spirit and law, between gospel and law. Church legislation in its modern form takes account of the traditional distinction between the visible and the invisible aspects of the church, between the church as founded by Christ and the church as it exists in history, between the church as the entity of salvation and the church in its earthly manifestation. The more the church corresponds to its spiritual foundation, the more important the application of theological criteria, the proclamation of the word, the administration of the sacraments and worship.

The distinction between laity and clergy plays an important role in the self-understanding of the church. In the Roman Catholic Church the clergy is *ex divina institutione*, a class apart, clearly distinct from the laity. By virtue of their ordination and governing power only members of the clergy can exercise certain official ecclesiastical functions. The Reformation abolished this distinction and the inequality among members which it creates. The relationship between the congregation as the community of believers and the office of the ministry replaced the Roman two-class system. Church legislation no longer focuses on the function of the hierarchy and hierarchical structures, but on the congregation and the role of the ministry of the word and the sacraments.

The question of who exercises governing power in the churches, the *potestas ecclesiastica,* is also replied to differently. In the Roman Catholic Church the governing power embraces two domains – one originating from *ordination,* the other from *jurisdiction.* The former has a sacramental character; the latter resides with the pope in matters regarding the universal church, *ex institutione divina,* and in all other cases depends on a nomination, either in the form of a *missio canonica* or a delegation. Ordination, which is lifelong, can be restricted or suspended by competent authorities, who also have the power to revoke the faculty of jurisdiction. Those who possess the power of jurisdiction also have legislative, judicial and judiciary authority.

In the churches of the Reformation, ordained ministers, who alone are entitled to proclaim the word and administer the sacraments, have limited leadership. The congregation itself is in charge of the government of its members. It has legislative and juridical power within the context of general civil law systems and of the church's constitution and its specific confession of faith.

Several forms and ways of exercising church power exist in territorial or national churches within the framework of the various confessions of faith. The most important of these are episcopal, synodal and consistorial power. A distinction must be made between church officials with an executive function, and the synod, which has legislative and judicial power. The role and function of bishops in the churches of the Reformation varies, but in general they are subordinated to synods.

It is a generally accepted doctrine that a person becomes a member of the body of Christ through baptism and is incorporated in the one holy, catholic and apostolic church, initiated into the life of a visibly constituted church. The Augsburg Confession affirms that baptism is necessary to receive grace and that children should be baptized. The Heidelberg Catechism asserts that baptism, which washes the soul and produces purity and grace, is the means by which a person, also a child, becomes a member of the church of Christ. Thanks to the ecumenical movement, most Christian churches recognize the legitimacy of baptism in one another's churches.

Membership of a visible church involves rights and duties. The Roman Catholic Code of Canon Law stipulates that "by baptism one is incorporated into the Church of Christ and is constituted a person in it with duties and rights which are proper to Christians, in keeping with their condition to the extent that they are in ecclesiastical communion, unless a legitimately issued sanction stands in the way" (Canon 96).

In many countries membership of a visible Christian church also has juridical consequences linked with citizenship. For example, church tax is an essential part of the revenue system of some countries; and resigning church membership may have juridical consequences with regard to state laws. There may also be mixed cases which involve both church and state laws, such as the office of professor of theology. In many countries concordats or specific agreements between churches and states regulate the juridical demands and privileges of both partners.

2. Two international consultations

During the 1970s, the Department of Studies of the Lutheran World Federation organized two international consultations in connection with a study on "Church Law and Polity in Lutheran Churches."[2] Since much of what was discussed applies to all Reformation churches in modern democratic societies, it is worthwhile to look more closely at some of its conclusions.

The report acknowledges that

> for many Lutherans the term "church law" is forbidding. Hence, this international study process on questions of church structures, polity, organization and orders often threatened to fail as interest waned at the mere mention of the concept of church law. However, as soon as we defined more precisely which questions and issues this notion encompasses, attention revived.

To some extent, this lukewarm initial response may have reflected the traditional Lutheran suspicion that "church law" is a contradiction in terms. Nevertheless, an immense variety of church legislation has emerged from the diverse histories of the Lutheran churches; and issues of governance continue to confront church leaders at various levels. In the end, says the report, "the participants were surprised by the amount of agreement which was apparent in the way the questions were posed, though the situations in which the questions arose were very different".

The report observes that the separation of state and church has created a great degree of uniformity in the domains in which the churches can freely operate and has contributed to an increasing similarity among church legislations. One of the aims of the Lutheran consultations was to analyze the rights and duties of state and church, so as to elaborate a juridically justified platform of collaboration between them.

Before the first consultation a preparatory task force agreed that church law should be divided into two categories: (1) laws which regulate the internal life of the church and (2) laws which apply to the church in its relation to society, that is, legal norms under which the church must function as a legal entity. Concerning the former, eight areas were singled out:

- the relationship between ministry (pastor) and congregation on the local level and, by analogy, on the various levels of church structure, and in this connection, the problem of the concept of *ius divinum*;
- the relationship between the local congregation and central structures;
- the exercise of pastoral oversight *(episcopé)* and the tension between such pastoral oversight and administrative and representative functions;
- church membership, both from a theological point of view (in relation to baptism) and from a legal or disciplinary point of view (the problem of termination of church membership in the light of the permanent validity of baptism);
- church discipline (of both lay persons and clergy);
- the importance of the confessions of faith and the concept of confessional subscription;
- responsibility for worship and spiritual life;
- qualifications for ecclesiastical elections and voting.

Concerning the church's external relations, the consultations gave considerable attention to issues related to religious liberty – its content, limitations on it, the freedom of the church to carry out its full mission in areas such as education, and the relation of the privileges of the church to unwarranted discrimination by the state on behalf of the church. Also examined were the theoretical and legal aspects of church-state cooperation (as in education and the social welfare sphere) and the analogies to secular law in the church's polity, by-laws and procedures.

An analysis of the statement on religious liberty by the WCC's New Delhi assembly (1961) led to six conclusions:

1. Individual religious liberty finds expression in such collective actions as worship and other congregational activities.

2. The church has the right and the freedom to engage in its fundamental activities – the proclamation and teaching of the gospel – without approval from or special supervision by the state. This freedom includes operating schools, youth organizations, hospitals and welfare institutions.

3. Every religious community has in principle the right not only to regulate its own affairs, but also to settle conflicts through courts or procedures of its own.

4. Religious activities may be subject to restrictions necessary to ensure public safety, morality and health, but it is essential that such restrictions do not discriminate against religious activities as such. All laws must be seen in the light of the human right to religious liberty and interpreted accordingly.

5. Since the fellowship of the church is ecumenical, the church's task therefore is global; and Christian activities cannot come to a standstill at national borders. Religious communities should have the freedom to send personnel, money and supplies to foreign countries in support of religious activities. The communities to which these are directed should have the freedom to receive and accept them. In this area the churches have no principles of international law to fall back on, except for provisions which may be contained in treaties.

6. It is consistent with religious liberty for the state to cooperate with religious communities by supporting initiatives of common interest. In the special case of the maintenance of buildings used by religious communities which have a special historical and cultural significance for the entire community, the state should cover a fair share of the costs.

If the church needs a legal structure, where does it turn? What are the sources for church law? The first Lutheran consultation noted that both Scripture and the confessions of faith contain many references to legal procedures. Just as society over the centuries has adopted many legal norms rooted in Scripture which were formulated in church laws, so, too, the church today should be free to adopt legal norms of present society for regulating its own internal life. For example, the ordination of women to the ministry means the acceptance in church law of the principle of equality between the sexes, in analogy with secular law. In a sense, the principle that in Christ there is neither male nor female has permeated modern society through the Enlightenment and liberalism; and it now comes back to the churches in the form of the norm of equality of all human beings.

The concept of the interrelation of church law and state law can also be applied to the question of democracy in the church. Total democracy would create many difficulties for churches: questions of faith, for instance, cannot be decided by majority vote. Yet churches are expected to promote democracy in modern society. Can they do so if they do not practise democracy in their own life and structures?

The consultation agreed that no universally valid rules or principles can be set forth here. In its practical relationships with the state, a church depends on the basic order established between the two partners, and on the possibilities offered by the civil and public laws of its particular state.

Regarding the laws that regulate internal church life, the general conviction was that churches are free to provide themselves with norms and rules of ecclesiastical law within the framework of the state. The ecclesiastical laws should encompass the preaching of the word and the administration of the sacraments, the office of the ministry and the communion of the baptized, the mandate to mission and responsibility for the world. Because church members are also citizens, and because the principles of civil and public laws often guarantee justice, equality and responsibility, there is no objection to the church's adopting forms of secular laws, but only after critical examination of whether it corresponds to the church's mission and task.

There was consensus that the priesthood of all believers provides a theological basis for applying democratic norms and rules regarding votes and elections in the church. For this reason, baptism is the essential requirement and membership of a congregation or larger confessional community a further one. Indeed, the priesthood of all believers is the theological foundation of responsible cooperation by all members of the church. The ministry of the word and the congregation are correlative entities; their correlation defines and limits the application of the democratic principles in the church.

Considering this principle, the proportions of ordained and lay people in the various church boards and agencies can be structured according to rational considerations. Ecclesiastical tradition, the needs of the church (which vary according to its situation in society) and the appropriate divisions of responsibility can all be taken into account.

The second consultation in this study, which included participants from Europe, North America, Latin America and Africa, concentrated on such issues as church membership and the role of the Lutheran World Federation as a switchboard for members of the Lutheran confession.

The equality of all members was emphasized and any differentiation rejected. It was noted that a major problem in church discipline is that not all members are prepared to accept the restriction of their citizen rights and to change their conduct accordingly. Furthermore, participants at the consultation said the juridical responsibilities and duties of office-holders should be formulated more exactly. Measures of church discipline, including excommunication, should be understood as *poena med-icinalis;* church law differs at this point from civil law.

Implicitly, the universal priesthood in which one of the baptized members is delegated to exercise the ministry includes the conviction that the congregation has an electoral responsibility. Through voting and electing, the congregation gives reality to part of the universal priesthood bestowed upon it. This Christian justification of the right to vote and hold office proves that ecclesiastical office is in this sense independent of state laws or state interference.

There was a long discussion of the relationship between the local congregation and the general church, particularly about the existence of supra-congregational laws and the obligation of the local congregations to follow decisions made at the supra-congregational level. Theologically, the local congregation and the general church should be understood as *ecclesia.* The participants concluded that the church at the national level as well as all its subdivisions form an outer and inner unity. All must accomplish the same mission; and all members of a local congregation are also members of a national and general church. Ordination today is vested in the church at the highest level, either in virtue of its own direct right or because congregations have delegated their right; ordination is carried out by, and is valid for, the general church. Hence, it is not repeated in case of a change of area or service. Moreover, a Catholic priest who converts to a Protestant church does not have to be reordained – although commitment to its confessions of faith is imperative.

In conclusion that participants stated:

> The member churches of the Lutheran World Federation are called upon to deepen their community among each other and to labour for the unity of the whole of Christendom. Organizational and corporate unions and the union of churches in a particular region can serve such ends. The fact that churches in a region are divided organizations may, in the light of certain social circumstances, demand consolidation, also from spiritual and theological points of view, if that is related to the church's credibility as a witnessing and ministering community. The premise for the union of churches is pulpit and altar fellowship. Religious freedom includes the right of the churches to enter into relationships across national borders and to foster a community, including that of an institutional nature.

3. Premises for updating church legislation

In updating church legislation, Lutheran and Reformed theologians and church lawyers have taken as starting point the qualitative difference of church law from all other legal systems. Its uniqueness stems from its

Christocentric character and its fundamental rootage in Scripture and confessions of faith. Religious freedom should be considered the foundation of laws regulating the internal life of the churches and their fulfilment of their mission in the world. This principle of religious freedom should guarantee the proclamation of the word and the administration of the sacraments.

Through baptism a person becomes a full member of a congregation or community of believers – with all the duties and rights this entails. In virtue of the universal priesthood of all believers, all members have the right to vote; election is an individual contribution to the life of the congregation. The principle of democracy affirms even more strongly the equality of all members. The congregation and the ordained ministry are two correlative entities. The congregation names its pastor who is responsible for the proclamation of the word and the administration of the sacraments. The highest ecclesiastical authority resides with the congregation, which exercises this authority in general through a synod. For the sake of discipline within the congregation and the observance of rules of faith and moral behaviour, the congregation has the right to coerce offending members.

The legal systems regulating external relationships with civil authorities and the state will differ from nation to nation. In this respect "established churches" are a special case. However, state interference is diminishing, and the independence of the churches, especially with regard to their internal life, is steadily growing. There are countries with domains of common interest which call for special agreements. But it is part of the principle of religious freedom that churches be permitted to set up their own religious education and medical and social welfare systems. In nations which have introduced democratic principles for the various sectors of public life, the adoption of civil laws is in many cases preferable to this, because they generally guarantee justice, equality and democracy.

Under the influence of social changes and especially in the wake of the ecumenical movement, the local church, congregation or community comes to see itself as part of a larger territorial entity. In many ways, the rise of national churches with national governing and administrative bodies marked the end of the traditional territorial church system. Delegated by the local congregation, the highest executive authority resided with these new national organs, while the synod remained the highest legislative and judicial authority from the local level to the national level. The national synods were vested with the authority to ordain candidates to the ministry. All the while, openness to relationships beyond national and confessional borders intensified.

Religious freedom includes the right of the churches to enter into relationships with other churches across national borders. Not only churches of the same confession but also churches of different confessions have entered into pulpit and altar fellowship. These elements should be taken up as building blocks for an international law system for present and future ecumenical realities. As we have seen, the 1974 Outline urged that "the different legal systems of the churches should be brought closer to one another". But although developments in society and in and among the churches have created positive premises for such movement, an ecumenical law system remains a distant prospect.

NOTES

1 See Rau, et al., eds, *Das Recht der Kirche*, 3 vols, 1994-1997; Martin Honecker, "Kirchenrecht", in *Theologische Realenenzyklopädie*, Vol. 18, Berlin and New York, Walter de Gruyer, 1989, pp.713-49.
2 Cf. Albert Stein, "Herrschaft Christi und Geschwisterliche Gemeinde: Barmen, Dahlem und ihre Rezeption", in *Das Recht der Kirche*, Vol. 2, pp.273-317. For the texts of the Lutheran reports, see *Church Law and Polity in Lutheran Churches: Reports of the International Consultations Järvenpää (1970) and Baastad (1977)*, Geneva, Department of Studies of the Lutheran World Federation, 1979.

CHAPTER 8

New Perspectives

As new perspectives for the ecumenical movement emerge from developments in the various confessional families, their juridical consequences will have to be taken into consideration in the updating of church legislation.

1. The Orthodox church

a. *Renewal of the canonical tradition.* Some Orthodox historians have insisted that Orthodox canon law, comprising one thousand canons, should be updated. Timothy Ware, for example, writes: "Many of the canons are difficult or impossible to apply, and have fallen widely into disuse. When and if a new general council of the church is assembled, one of its chief tasks may well be the revision and clarification of canon law."[1]

In a recent substantial study of Orthodox canon law,[2] Vlassios Phidas of the University of Athens lists its principal sources as (1) canons issued by the seven ecumenical councils between 325 and 787, which represent the universal church; (2) canons which originate from local synods and were subsequently ratified by ecumenical councils; and (3) canons formulated by the fathers of the church. Orthodox canon law, which has never been codified, is not prescriptive in the sense of anticipating situations, but corrective, responding to situations once they have occurred.

Phidas acknowledges that many theologians want to change canon law with its "antiquated" canons. They do not see canon law as an instrument of pastoral care. However, he argues, it is incorrect to confuse "the spirit of the canons", their profound meaning, with their formulation, which has taken a specific shape corresponding to an historical situation. The canons formulate the experience of the church at a certain point in history. While we live in changed historical situations, the mission of the church remains the same, although in a different way.

Tradition always expresses the ecclesial conscience – which is not bound to a certain time – with regard to the truth which the church must offer in fullness at all times. In this sense, the old texts of the canons must receive a new form. But this means not that the spirit of the canons should be essentially changed, abolished or violated, but that it must be revived in a new canonical formulation. Only in this way can the message of salvation, the entire sacred tradition and the presence of the Holy Spirit continue its historical and traditional road. In other words, a new elaboration of the canons must represent an authentic witness to the continuity of the history of salvation. "The message of salvation in Christ carries the mark of historicity of its experience, and it is lived without ceasing as a tradition of the past, as an adaptation in present time and as a road towards the future, towards the eschaton."

Respect for the canonical tradition is related not only to the essence of the spirit of the canons, but also to the text itself and its historical formulation. The Orthodox church seeks to be faithful to the historical conjunction between the spirit and the text. However, the actual formulation of the canons as they have come to us is certainly not an absolute and essential element of the Orthodox tradition. The Orthodox church feels free to interpret and actualize the contents of Christ's revelation according to the needs of the faithful.

This interpretation of the canons is presently accepted by all autocephalous Orthodox churches. It would be wrong to introduce a codification of Orthodox canon law, which would mean maintaining the original text or formulation of the canons along with preserving their spirit. "The Orthodox church aims at the renewal of the canonical tradition in the context of both the unity of its spiritual mission and of the diversity of the continually changing spiritual needs of the believers." The canons which enjoy the authority of the ecumenical councils reveal, in any case, the authentic conscience of the church as it develops under the guidance of the Holy Spirit.

b. *Church-state relations.* For the Orthodox tradition, church and state are two "perfect societies", each with its own aims and means. The relationship between church and state is a delicate issue in the Orthodox tradition and must be seen in the wider context of the relations of the church with the world. As Phidas summarizes it,

> the fundamental principles of the Orthodox tradition derive on the one hand from the ecclesiological teaching concerning the local church and on the other hand from the church's pastoral choice to serve the nation in the context of the spiritual mission of the church in the world. The political theology of the Orthodox church has been moulded on the principle of clearly distinguishing the parallelism and equality between the ecclesiastical and civil authorities... The theoretical principles of the political theology of the Orthodox church stem from its teaching on the strictly spiritual nature of its mission in the world.[3]

The secular nature of the modern state prevents it from being sensitive to the independence of the church's spiritual mission. Indeed, the church is strongly affected by anti-clerical or anti-religious currents, hidden or open, in ideological systems which cherish the dream of seeing the church totally or partially lose its social influence. The traditional schema deriving both church and state from divine authority has given way to the principle of the sovereignty of the people. In the name of this principle, states often exercise absolute authority, but a state may never ignore the right of citizens to practise their religion.

In any case, the church must insist on its doctrinal principles and adapt as well as possible to the circumstances, proposing a minimum of agreement on issues involving both church and state, such as education, marriages between Christians, the civil status of the clergy, church institutions and church property. Since church-state relations are no longer based on the fundamental principle of two independent powers but on the sovereignty of the people and human rights, the model of "symphony" or separation between church and state has been replaced by the principle of state supremacy. But the forceful resistance of the church to this new model poses again the issue of a symphony of practical collaboration in the service of the people.

While a new synthesis may grow out of this renewed collaboration, it is the task of the church to watch with critical eyes the evolution of the political situation. It should be noted that in the past it was the church that was concerned with the cultivation of good relations with the state, while today it is the state that aims at good and fruitful relations with the church.

2. The Roman Catholic Church: the quest for decentralization

As a result of the Second Vatican Council, the Roman Catholic Church has two different ecclesiologies available. The hierarchical institution headed by the bishop of Rome, who enjoys a primacy that turns him into an absolute monarch over the universal church, continues on the foundation laid by the First Vatican Council. This calls for a strong central administration in the Roman Curia. The second ecclesiology has made Catholics aware that they constitute the people of God. It envisages a church that is first and foremost a communion, whose essential elements are collegiality, participation and subsidiarity. The consequence of this new model is overall decentralization.

With the global extent of the Roman Catholic Church bringing increased cultural differentiation, the exercise of the papal ministry as a central authority becomes difficult to understand. It leads to conflicts with particular or local churches and with regional or continental churches. Those responsible for a strongly centralized Church are generally convinced that the second model, which aims at reduction of Vatican centralization, means a weakening of the authority of the Petrine office. They fear not only the reinforcement of the power of the bishops but also the exercise of the rights of particular churches – whether nationally or regionally – to play a collaborative role in the government of the universal church.[4] The Second Vatican Council undermined the Vatican centralization by supplying the basic elements for a church structured as a decentralized communion of churches. But for the time being there remains a juxtaposition of different priorities founded on different ecclesiologies.

The Second Vatican Council's Dogmatic Constitution on the Church (*Lumen Gentium*) reintroduced the people of God "as the fundamental and constitutive element of the Church". Chapter 2 describes the characteristics of the new people of God: they are baptized believers, all of equal dignity, living from the Spirit, free children of God. Hence, the church is built up from below. The one and only Catholic Church comes into being "in and from the local churches" (para. 23). The Church is therefore called "the body of churches".

No longer are the bishops vicars of the Roman pontiff, as they were in the times after the Council of Trent, but they exercise authority of their own. *Lumen Gentium* stipulates that by virtue of their ordination bishops receive the powers to sanctify, teach and govern their diocese. "They exercise an authority which is proper to them... This power, therefore, is not destroyed by the supreme and universal power." The Code of Canon Law affirms that "a diocesan bishop in the diocese committed to him possesses all the ordinary, proper and immediate power which is required for the exercise of his pastoral office" (Canon 381).

Neighbouring particular churches frequently form an ecclesiastical province to promote common pastoral activity. The Second Vatican Council decree *Christus Dominus* reaffirmed the existence of national episcopal conferences. The Code of Canon Law (Canons 447-458) states that their primary aim is to "jointly exercise certain pastoral functions". The Apostolic See is in charge of the institution of national episcopal conferences. Their statutes require the approval of the Holy See. They may issue general decrees only in cases prescribed by common law or determined by the Apostolic See. Reports of their plenary sessions are to be sent to the Apostolic See. The competence of individual diocesan bishops remains intact.

From this, the limits on the authority of the national episcopal conferences are evident: in short, the Vatican exercises permanent control over their activities. This was officially reinforced by an apostolic letter

of Pope John Paul II in July 1998,[5] which limits the authority of the episcopal conference even further. In the conferences, the bishops do not
exercise the same authority as they do as members of the college of bishops for the universal church. Furthermore, they should not approve provisions which they consider to be against the interest of their own diocese. In some cases, the episcopal conference constitutes an authentic
magisterium; declarations on faith and morals require its unanimous
approval.

After the Second Vatican Council, Catholic theologians such as Karl
Rahner, E. Schillebeeckx and Küng pointed at ambiguities in the documents and at the coexistence of two ecclesiologies. The Vatican took the
necessary measures to reinforce the traditional model: the synod of bishops was downgraded into an advisory board. Bishops who were more
inclined to follow the traditional ecclesiology were systematically
appointed at the head of dioceses. The Congregation for the Doctrine of
the Faith sent a warning to theologians suspected of not showing due
respect for the primacy of the bishop of Rome; and in October 1998 it
issued a special document on the primacy of the pope, to counter any
possibility of developing a differing personal view on this.[6] In effect, the
Roman Curia took over the task which belonged to the College of Bishops of governing the universal church. Neither the Second Vatican Council definition that each bishop should be solicitous for the entire church
nor the principles of participation, collegiality and subsidiarity have
been applied.

The Vatican strategy has provoked a serious crisis in the church. An
increasing number of Catholics are quietly ignoring Vatican rules about
divorce, remarriage and eucharistic discipline and its teachings on
human sexuality. Numerous people have left the Catholic Church to join
Evangelical and Pentecostal bodies. The New Age movement has also
attracted many Catholics. Throughout the world, church affiliation is felt
to be voluntary rather than obligatory. Although a shortage of priests is
hampering normal pastoral activity, the Vatican maintains obligatory
celibacy and continues to exclude women from the priesthood.

Mention should also be made here of the membership of the Roman
Catholic Church in national councils of churches. Fifty-five of these now
have official Roman Catholic membership and are at the same time officially related to the World Council of Churches. Neither the WCC nor
the Vatican has said how this situation can be solved juridically.

3. The Joint Declaration on justification

The Joint Declaration on the Doctrine of Justification signed by representatives of the Lutheran World Federation and the Pontifical Coun-

cil for Promoting Christian Unity on Reformation Sunday, 31 October 1999, was the result of more than thirty years of dialogue between the two partners.[7]

As the Declaration points out, the doctrine of justification was of central importance for the Lutheran Reformation. It was considered the "first and chief article" of Christian doctrine and the ruler and judge over all other doctrines. For the Reformation churches, the differences in contents and wording of this doctrine from Roman Catholic teaching made justification the crux of all disputes. Doctrinal condemnations were put forward, both in the Lutheran confessions and by the Council of Trent.

Now, the Declaration affirms, the two partners are able to articulate a "common understanding of our justification by God's grace through faith in Christ". The Declaration does not encompass the entire Lutheran or Catholic teaching on justification, but it does put forward a consensus on basic doctrinal truths and shows that the remaining differences are no longer the occasion for doctrinal condemnations. "The Joint Declaration rests on the conviction that in overcoming the earlier controversial questions and doctrinal condemnations... our churches have come to new insights... Developments have taken place that require the churches to see the decisive questions and condemnations in a new light."

Using "insights of recent biblical studies" and "modern investigation of the history of theology and dogma", the Joint Declaration formulates a consensus on "basic truths concerning the doctrine of justification" in the light of which the 16th-century doctrinal condemnations no longer apply. The fundamental agreement is summarized as follows:

> In faith we together hold the conviction that justification is the work of the triune God. The Father sent his Son into the world to save sinners. The foundation and presupposition of justification is the incarnation, death and resurrection of Christ. Justification thus means that Christ himself is our righteousness, in which we share through the Holy Spirit in accord with the will of the Father. Together we confess: By grace alone, in faith in Christ's saving work and not because of any merit on our part, we are accepted by God and receive the Holy Spirit, who renews our hearts while equipping and calling us to good works.
>
> All people are called by God to salvation in Christ. Through Christ alone are we justified, when we receive this salvation in faith. Faith is itself God's gift, through the Holy Spirit who works through word and sacrament in the community of believers and who, at the same time, leads believers into that renewal of life which God will bring to completion in eternal life... The doctrine of justification is, therefore, more than just one part of Christian doctrine. It stands in essential relation to all truths of faith, which are to be seen as internally related to each other.

The Declaration goes on to explicate the common understanding of justification in terms of "Human Powerlessness and Sin in Relation to Justification", "Justification as Forgivenness of Sins and Making Righteous", "The Justified as Sinners" and "Law and Gospel". The text on law and gospel emphasizes that Christ has fulfilled the law and by his death and resurrection has overcome law as a way to salvation. God's commandments retain their validity for the justified and Christ has by his teaching and example expressed God's will, which is a standard for the conduct of the justified. Lutherans, furthermore, state that the distinction and right ordering of law and gospel is essential for the understanding of justification. Catholics can say that Christ is not a lawgiver in the manner of Moses. The righteous are bound to observe God's commandments, but they do not thereby deny that through Jesus Christ God has mercifully promised to his children the grace of eternal life.

After explicating "The Assurance of Salvation" and "The Good Works of the Justified", the Declaration concludes with a list of areas in which further clarification is needed: the relationship between the Word of God and church doctrine, ecclesiology, authority in the church, ministry, the sacraments and the relation between justification and social ethics.

A week after the LWF Council approved the Joint Declaration on 16 June 1998, the Vatican response arrived. It appeared to cast doubt on the Vatican's willingness to state that the 16th-century condemnations no longer applied to Lutheran teaching. Extended negotiations with the Vatican led to the announcement that the Declaration would be signed in October 1999.

Quite apart from its substantive content, the Declaration is a breakthrough in that it marks the first time that the Vatican has accepted in an authoritative form the results of a bilateral dialogue with another confession and has affirmed the agreement in a formal signing ceremony. To close the divergences of the past on the most fundamental point of the Christian faith and to enter into new permanent relationships obviously has juridical consequences. The new legal status between the two confessions should equally be an important question for further clarification. Ultimately it is not only the LWF and the Roman Catholic Church who are involved in this common agreement; it is also of fundamental importance for the other confessions originating from the Reformation, particularly the Reformed and Anglican confessions.

4. *The Gift of Authority*

Already in 1968, Archbishop of Canterbury Michael Ramsey and Pope Paul VI initiated a theological dialogue between the Anglican

Communion and the Roman Catholic Church. The Anglican and Roman Catholic International Commission (ARCIC) in 1981 issued a Final Report containing agreed statements on the eucharist, ministry and authority. The text on authority included many points on which both sides could agree, but it also identified important areas for further study and discussion: the relationship between Scripture, Tradition and the exercise of teaching authority, collegiality, conciliarity, the role of the laity in decision-making and the Petrine ministry of universal primacy. On 12 May 1999, ARCIC offered the results of its research, study and prayer in a report entitled *The Gift of Authority*.8 Its presupposition is that full visible communion of the two churches entails the acceptance of a common authority, which in turn requires a shared understanding of what authority in the church means and of how it should be exercised.

There are some important commonalities between *The Gift of Authority* and the Joint Declaration on Justification. Both concern the justification and elevation of human nature through Christ's redeeming grace: the Declaration focuses on how this occurs in the life of the justified individual, while *The Gift of Authority* studies the working of grace within the whole believing community. Both texts are fundamental for the progress of the ecumenical movement. The importance of both goes beyond the confessions directly involved. In a sense, the authority text is a response to Pope John Paul II's Encyclical Letter *Ut Unum Sint*. It seeks to contribute to the common search for primacy a special concern for the healing of divisions between all Christian churches.

The key to understanding the document is the image Paul uses in 2 Corinthians 1:19-20 – the "Yes" to humanity in Jesus Christ, which explains the ultimate purpose of authority in the churches and which enables their members to respond with a faithful "Amen" as they walk Christ's way. The individual believer's "Amen" to Christ equally involves an "Amen" of the believing community, thus relating the faith of the individual to that of the community.

According to the report, Tradition makes the witness of the apostolic community present in the church; and the Spirit continues to teach the church, reminding it of what Christ did and said, making present the fruits of his redemptive work. Within the Tradition, Scripture occupies a unique and normative place as the written witness to God's "Yes". The gospel can be fully understood only within the church, the community which has to hand on the apostolic Tradition.

Fresh recourse to Tradition in a new situation is the means by which God's revelation in Christ is recalled. "The people of God as a whole" is the bearer of the living Tradition. "The Holy Spirit works through all members of the community." The report speaks of the *sensus fidei* in every Christian who is incorporated into the life of the church – an intuition and capacity for spiritual discernment formed by worship and life in community as a faithful believer. Every member contributes to the formation of the *sensus fidelium,* through which the church as a whole remains faithful to Christ.

Those who exercise *episcopé* in the body of Christ must not be separated from the "symphony" of the whole people of God. The report connects the charism and function of *episcopé* with the "ministry of memory" which constantly renews the church in hope. This is the ministry exercised by the bishop and ordained persons as they proclaim the word, administer the sacraments and take part in exercising discipline.

The report also notes the link between the *sensus fidelium* and the ministry of memory. No local church participating in the living Tradition can regard itself as sufficient. It needs forms of synodality to manifest its communion with the other local churches and to sustain all of them in fidelity to the gospel. Within the whole body of the church, the college of bishops is to exercise the ministry of memory: the bishops are to discern and provide a teaching that can be trusted as an expression of the certain truth of God. In specific circumstances, those entrusted with the ministry of oversight may together, with the assistance of the Holy Spirit, come to a judgment in faithfulness to Scripture and consistent with the apostolic Tradition. This is what is meant by infallible teaching, which is at the service of the church's indefectibility. The exercise of teaching with authority requires the participation of the whole body of believers, and this participation is expressed in the *sensus fidelium.*

The demands of church life call for a specific exercise of *episcopé* at the service of the whole church. Historically, it is the bishop of Rome who has exercised this ministry – which has been the source of difficulties and misunderstandings among the churches. It is the duty of the episcopal college, bound in succession to the apostles, to maintain the church in the truth; and the solemn definitions by the bishop of Rome must always be pronounced within, never outside of, the college of bishops. The teaching of the bishop of Rome is the teaching of the whole episcopal college and thus of its local communities. It is therefore "the wholly reliable teaching of the whole Church that is operative in the judgment of the universal primate". In solemnly formulating definitions, the universal primate must discern and declare, under the guidance of the Holy Spirit, in fidelity to Scripture and Tradition, the authentic faith of the whole church, that is, the faith as it was lived from the beginning. Such solemn and authoritative affirmations of the faith are expressed by ecumenical councils or made explicit by the bishop of Rome: "The reception of the primacy of the bishop of Rome entails the recognition of the

Disciples, Baptists, Brethren). Many united churches are products of the 20th-century ecumenical movement, with the majority emerging since the second world war in former colonized nations where confessional divisions have little historical significance and the need for common Christian witness is keenly felt.[10]

At the 1996 meeting of the Faith and Order Commission in Moshi, Tanzania, Martin Cressey identified the main characteristic of church unions as a level of mutual commitment, community and accountability among the constituent churches so strong that it cannot be expressed through plans for "partnership" or mutual recognition, but must take the form of full structural union. Diversity is "recognized" to the radical extent of being integrated within a single ecclesial body – with all this implies theologically and institutionally. Thus, "to unite is to accept responsibility for one another in the fullest sense". A key issue identified in the discussion was how different ecclesial forms, each bearing its full theological seriousness and weight of tradition, can be brought together within the same ecclesial body.[11]

Beginning in 1967 an international consultation of united and uniting churches has been convened regularly to explore the challenges facing these churches and the special contribution they have to make to the ecumenical movement.[12]

The existence of united and uniting churches is a permanent plea to other churches to overcome their divisions, emphasizing that Christians cannot rest content with their continuing failure to achieve full visible unity. They approach the still-divided churches with new insights on the one eucharistic fellowship and on the need for healing. At the same time, they feel the need to redefine their own identity. United and uniting churches believe that their particular contribution to the mission of the whole church comes in providing a model of diversity within unity in communities of increasing pluralism.

Obstacles to church union often result from an emphasis on power, the attitude of certain ministers, and especially the accent on separate identities. The issue of what form of *episcopé* to adopt remains divisive. The report of the 1995 consultation of united and uniting churches states that churches are currently in an "ecumenical winter", which has come along with a resurgence of confessionalism that is in part a denial of the ecumenical vision, in part a desire to return to the certainties of traditional teaching.

A sign of hope for Christian unity was the Leuenberg agreement between Reformation churches in Europe. The Porvoo Statement marks the visible unity of Lutheran churches from Nordic and Baltic countries and Anglican churches in the British Isles. Similar agreements are being specific ministry of the universal primate. We believe that this is a gift to be received by all the churches."

The Gift of Authority concludes with an acknowledgment that while Anglicans and Roman Catholics are already facing these issues, it may well take some time to resolve them; "however, there is no turning back in our journey towards full ecclesial communion". Initial reactions to the report, especially from the Anglican side, were not altogether positive. But the fact that *The Gift of Authority* does not attribute any jurisdiction or juridical power to the bishop of Rome led one Anglican member of the Commission to say:

> We dream together of a new kind of papal primacy that will even now help to uphold the legitimate diversity of traditions and will welcome and protect theological enquiry and other forms of the search for truth, so that their results may enrich and strengthen human wisdom and the church's faith. As an Anglican, I had no difficulty endorsing those statements.[9]

The outcome of the reception of *The Gift of Authority* will in any case have a serious impact on the legal relationships between the two churches.

5. The juridical impact of united churches

United churches are national or regional churches formed by the union of two or more denominations – either within a single confessional family or from different confessional traditions – which were previously separated.

While there is no single model of united churches, four characteristics generally hold true. (1) United churches have achieved organic or structural union in the sense of being able to make common decisions on faith and order, mission and use of their resources. This distinguishes them from relationships of "full communion" between still-separated churches. (2) Unlike councils or federations of churches, united churches are worshipping faith communities with their own patterns of authorized ministry. (3) The context in which united churches seek to give expression to the gospel is that of the present ecumenical movement rather than that of inherited confessions. (4) The self-understanding of united churches is largely shaped by an intentional act of "uniting" through which a new church identity has been assumed.

Beyond these common elements, united churches exhibit great variety. Most are the outcome of decades of negotiation and planning, but some have come into being quickly. A few are episcopally ordered because of Anglican participation, others are formed by the union of Reformation churches (Presbyterians, Methodists, Congregationalists, worked out in South Africa, India and North America. In the Netherlands a process is on the way towards the union of the Netherlands Reformed Church, the Reformed Churches in the Netherlands and the Evangelical Lutheran Church in the Kingdom of the Netherlands.

The Faith and Order Outline of 1974 clearly states that updating church legislation does not mean establishing a uniform juridical pattern everywhere. There is no single legal model that is suitable for all cases. United and uniting churches display elements which can contribute to a broad legal model: the churches unite in a single ecclesial body with all its theological and institutional implications. They take responsibility for one another in the fullest sense. They show how different ecclesial forms, each bearing its full seriousness and weight of tradition, can be brought together within one and the same ecclesial body.

But it is not enough simply to state the problem. As the 1974 Outline affirms:

> Steps must be taken to focus the attention of the churches upon it... We believe that the essential first step must be to devise a method by which individual churches can make a judgment, each upon its own situation... No situation is static, and we believe that an increased awareness of the juridical issues may help in changing the circumstances towards a gradual convergence to exercise a prophetic ministry and to be able to respond fully to the claims of the ecumenical commitment, both in the particular society and internationally.

NOTES

[1] Timothy Ware, *The Orthodox Church*, p.205.
[2] Vlassios I. Phidas, *Droit canon: une perspective orthodoxe,* Analecta Chambesiana 1, Geneva, Centre orthodoxe du Patriarchat oecuménique, 1998, pp.85-165.
[3] *Ibid.,* p.31.
[4] For a clear and succinct account of the present situation of the Roman Catholic Church, see Herman J. Pottmeyer, *Towards a Papacy in Communion: Perspectives from Vatican Councils I and II,* New York, Crossroad, 1998.
[5] English text in *L'Osservatore Romano*, English edition, 29 July 1998.
[6] Congregation for the Doctrine of the Faith: Il Primato del Successore di Pietro nel mistero della Chiesa, in *L'Osservatore Romano*, 31 Oct. 1998.
[7] For the text see *Information Service* of the Pontifical Council for Promoting Christian Unity, no. 98, 1998, pp.81-100.
[8] For the text see *ibid.,* no. 100, 1999, pp.17-29.
[9] John Muddiman, in *The Tablet,* 12 June 1999.
[10] Michael Kinnamon, "United and Uniting Churches", in Lossky, et al., eds, *Dictionary of the Ecumenical Movement*, pp.1032f.
[11] Alan Falconer, ed., *Faith and Order in Moshi: The 1996 Commission Meeting*, Faith and Order Paper no. 177, Geneva, WCC Publications, 1998, pp.203-205.
[12] For the report of the most recent consultation, the sixth (1995), see Thomas F. Best, ed., *Built Together: The Present Vocation of United and Uniting Churches*, Faith and Order Paper no. 174, Geneva, WCC, 1997, pp.6-31. Biennial surveys of church unions appear in *The Ecumenical Review;* most recently, vol. 52, no. 1, Jan. 2000, pp.3-45.

Bibliography

Abbott, Walter M., ed., *The Documents of Vatican II*, New York, Guild Press, 1966.

Aghiorgoussis, M., "The Dogmatic Tradition of the Orthodox Church", in *A Companion to the Greek Orthodox Church*, Fotios K. Litsas, ed., New York, Greek Orthodox Archdiocese of North and South America, 1984, pp.128-37.

Armstrong, Karen, *A History of God*, London, Heinemann, 1993.

Aymans, Winfried and Eichmann, Eduard, *Kanonisches Recht* – vol. 1: *Einleitende Grundfragen und Allgemeine Normen*, Paderborn, Schöningh, 1991.

Baptism, Eucharist and Ministry, Faith and Order Paper no. 111, Geneva, WCC, 1982.

Bent, A. van der, *Commitment to God's World: A Concise Critical Survey of Ecumenical Social Thought*, Geneva, WCC, 1995.

Bent, A. van der, "WCC Assemblies", in *Dictionary of the Ecumenical Movement*, pp.1090-1096 (see Lossky et al.).

Bertolino, Rinaldo, *Il nuovo diritto ecclesiale, tra coscienza dell'uomo e istituzione*, Turin, Giappichelli, 1989.

Best, Thomas F., ed., *Faith and Renewal: Reports and Documents of the Commission on Faith and Order, Stavanger 1985*, Faith and Order Paper no. 131, Geneva, WCC, 1985.

Bonhoeffer, D., *Gesammelte Schriften*, 6 vols, E. Bethge, ed., Münich, Kaiser, 1958-74.

Bonino, J. Míguez, "Ethics", in *Dictionary of the Ecumenical Movement*, p.364-69 (see Lossky et al.).

Brecht, M., *Martin Luther*, 3 vols, Stuttgart, Calwer, 1981-87.

Buchanan, C., "Anglican Communion", in *Dictionary of the Ecumenical Movement*, pp.18-20 (see Lossky et al.).

Calvin, J., *Institutes of the Christian Religion*, 2 vols, John T. McNeill, ed., Philadelphia, Westminster, 1960.

Calvin, J., *Institution de la religion chrestienne*, 4 vols, J. Pannier, ed., Paris, Belles Lettres, 1961.

Catéchisme du Concile de Trente, Bouère, France, Dominique Martin Morin, repr. 1984.

Catéchisme de l'Eglise catholique, Paris, Plon, 1992.

Cavelti, Urs Josef, "Katholisches Kirchenrecht", in *Ökumene im Kirchenrecht*, Fribourg, Universitätsverlag, 1996, pp.49-73.

Chadwick, H., "The Early Christian Community", in *The Oxford History of Christianity*, John McManners, ed., Oxford, Oxford UP, 1993, pp.21-61.

Chiba, S., Hunsberger, G., Ruiz, L., eds, *Christian Ethics in Ecumenical Context: Theology, Culture and Politics in Dialogue*, Grand Rapids MI, Eerdmans, 1995.

Church Law and Polity in Lutheran Churches: Reports of the International Consultations in Järvenpää and Baastad, Geneva, Lutheran World Federation, 1979.

Clément, Olivier, *Rome autrement: Une réflexion orthodoxe sur la papauté*, Paris, Desclée de Brouwer, 1997.

Code of Canon Law: Latin-English Edition, transl. prepared under the auspices of the Canon Law Society of America, Washington DC, Canon Law Society of America, 1983.

Codex juris canonici Pii X Pontificis Maximi jussu digestus Benedicti Papae XV auctoritate promulgatus/praefatione, fontium annotatione et indice analytico-alphabetico ab Petro Gasparri auctus, Rome, Typis Polyglottis Vaticanis, 1918.

Congregation for the Doctrine of the Faith, "Commentary on Concluding Formula of Professio Fidei", in *L'Osservatore Romano*, English ed., 15 July 1998.

Congregation for the Doctrine of the Faith, "The Primacy of the Successor of Peter in the Mystery of the Church", in *L'Osservatore Romano*, English ed., 18 Nov. 1998.

Congregation for the Doctrine of Faith, "Il Primato del Successore di Pietro nel mistero della Chiesa", in *L'Osservatore Romano*, 31 Oct. 1998.

"Constitution and Rules of the WCC", in *Gathered for Life: Official Report of the Sixth Assembly of the WCC Vancouver 1983*, David Gill, ed., Geneva, WCC Publications, 1983, pp.324-47.

Corecco, E. "Theologie des Kirchenrechts", in *Handbuch des katholischen Kirchenrechts*, pp.16-30 (see Listl et al.).

Cottret, B., *Calvin: Biographie*, Paris, J.C. Lattès, 1995.

"The Nicene Creed", "The Nicene-Constantinopolitan Creed", "The Apostles' Creed", "The Athanasian Creed", in *Enchiridion Symbolorum*, pp.1-6 (see Denzinger).

"The Creed of the Council of Trent", in *Enchiridion Symbolorum*, pp.6-9 (see Denzinger).

Cummings, D., transl., *The Rudder (Pedalion) of the Orthodox Church or All Sacred and Divine Canons*, Chicago, Orthodox Christian Educational Society, 1957.

Curran, Ch.E., *The Church and Morality: An Ecumenical and Catholic Approach*, Minneapolis, Fortress, 1993.

Decree on Ecumenism (Unitatis Redintegratio), in *The Documents of Vatican II*, pp.336-70 (see Abbott).

Dehren, D., "Kirchenverfassung und Kirchengesetz", in *Das Recht der Kirche*, pp.448-73 (see Rau et al.).

Denzinger, Heinrich, *Enchiridion Symbolorum*, Freiburg, Herder, 1953. English ed.: *The Church Teaches*, Rockford IL, Tan Books and Publ., 1973.

Derr, Th.S., *Barriers to Ecumenism: The Holy See and the World Council of Churches on Social Questions*, Maryknoll NY, Orbis, 1983.

Die Diskussion über Taufe, Eucharistie und Amt, 1982-1990: Stellungnahmen, Auswirkungen, Weiterarbeit, Frankfurt, Lembeck, 1990.

Doe, Norman, *Canon Law in the Anglican Communion: A Worldwide Perspective*, Oxford, Clarendon, 1998.

Dogmatic Constitution on the Church: Lumen Gentium, in *The Documents of Vatican II*, pp.14-101 (see Abbott).

Dombois, H., *Das Recht der Gnade: Ökumenisches Kirchenrecht*, 3 vols, Bielefeld, Luther Verlag, 1961-83.

Duffy, E. "The Popes, Theory and Fact", in *The Tablet*, 4 July 1998.

Ebneter, A., "Das neue katholische Kirchenrecht und die Ökumene", in *Ökumenische Rundschau*, 32, 1983, pp.461-76.

Ehler, Sidney Z. and Morall, John B., eds and transl., *Church and State through the Centuries: A Collection of Historic Documents*, London, Burns & Oates, 1954.

Erickson, J.H., *The Challenge of Our Past: Studies in Orthodox Canon Law and Church History*, Crestwood NY, St Vladimir's Seminary Press, 1991.

Fabricius, Cajus, ed., *Die Kirche von England: Ihr Gebetbuch, Bekenntnis und Kanonisches Recht*, Berlin, Walter de Gruyter, 1937.

Falconer, Alan, ed., "Faith and Order Work with United and Uniting Churches", in *Faith and Order in Moshi: The 1996 Commission Meeting*, Faith and Order Paper no. 177, Geneva, WCC Publications, 1998, pp.203-205.

Fatio, Olivier, ed., *Confessions et catéchismes de la foi réformée*, Genève, Labor et Fides, 1986.

"A Fellowship of Local Churches Truly United (1976)", in *Documentary History of Faith and Order, 1963-1993*, pp.69-75 (see Gassmann).

The Final Report of the Anglican-Roman Catholic International Commission, London, SPCK, 1982.

Fries, H., Rahner K., *Unity of the Churches: An Actual Possibility*, Philadelphia, Fortress, 1985.

Galvin, J.P. "Papal Primacy in Contemporary Roman Catholic Theology", in *Theological Studies*, Dec. 1986, pp.653-67.

Gassmann, Günther, ed., *Documentary History of Faith and Order 1963-1993*, Faith and Order Paper no. 159, Geneva, WCC Publications, 1993.

Gaudemet, J., *Eglise et cité: Histoire du droit canonique*, Paris, Cerf, Montchrestien, 1994.

Gaudemet, J., "Kirchenrecht", in *Theologische Realencyclopedie*, vol. XVIII, Berlin/New York, Walter de Gruyter, 1989, pp.713-34.

"The Gift of Authority: Authority in the Church III. Report of the Anglican Roman International Commission (ARCIC II)", in *Information Service of the Pontifical Council for Promoting Christian Unity*, no. 100, 1999, 1, pp.17-29.

Green, Th.J., "The Revised Code of Canon Law: Some Theological Issues", in *Theological Studies*, Dec. 1986, pp.617-52.

Gustafson, J.M., *Protestant and Roman Catholic Ethics: Prospects for Rapprochement*, Chicago, Univ. of Chicago Press, 1978.

Halkin, L.E., *Erasme parmi nous*, Paris, Fayard, 1987.

Häring, B., "My Hope for the Future of the Petrine Ministry", in *The Papacy and the People of God*, Gary MacEoin, ed., Maryknoll NY, Orbis, 1998, pp.16-21.

Hartvelt, G.P., *Symboliek: een beschrijving van kernen van christelijk belijden*, Kampen, Kok, 1991.

Huizing, P., "The Central Legal System and Autonomous Churches", in *Concilium*, June 1986, Edinburgh, T&T Clark, 1986, pp.23-31.

Pope John Paul II, "Apostolic Letter Issued Motu Proprio on the Theological and Juridical Nature of Episcopal Conferences", in *L'Osservatore Romano*, English ed., 29 July 1998.

Pope John Paul II, "Apostolic Letter Motu Proprio 'Ad Tuendam Fidem'", in *L'Osservatore Romano*, English ed., 15 July 1998.

Pope John Paul II, *"Ut Unum Sint": Encyclical Letter on Commitment to Ecumenism*, Vatican, Editrice Vaticana, 1995.

"Joint Declaration on the Doctrine of Justification: Lutheran World Federation and the Roman Catholic Church", in *Information Service of the Pontifical Council for Promoting Christian Unity*, no. 98, 1998, III, pp.81-100.

Joint Working Group between the Roman Catholic Church and the World Council of Churches, "The Ecumenical Dialogue on Moral Issues: Potential Sources of Common Witness or of Divisions", in *Seventh Report*, Geneva, WCC Publications, 1998, pp.31-42.

Kinnamon, Michael, ed., *Signs of the Spirit: Official Report of the Seventh Assembly of the World Council of Churches, Canberra 1991*, Geneva, WCC Publications, 1991.

Kinnamon, Michael, "United and Uniting Churches", in *Dictionary of the Ecumenical Movement*, pp.1032-1036 (see Lossky et al.).

Körtner, U.H.J., *Reformiert und ökumenisch: Brennpunkte reformierter Theologie in Geschichte und Gegenwart*, Innsbruck, Tyrolia, 1998.

Kuhn, K.-Ch., "Church Order instead of Church Law", in *Concilium*, 5, 1996, pp.29-39.

Le Gal, P., *Le droit canonique dans la pensée dialectique de Jean Calvin*, Fribourg, Ed universitaires, 1984.

L'Huillier, P., *The Church of the Ancient Councils: The Disciplinary Work of the First Four Ecumenical Councils*, New York, St Vladimir's Seminary Press, 1996.

Lienemann, W., "Partikularkirchen und ökumenische Bewegung", in *Das Recht der Kirche*, vol. II, pp.318-70 (see Rau et al.).

Listl, J., Müller, H., Schmitz, H., eds, *Handbuch des katholischen Kirchenrechts*, Regensburg, Friedrich Pustet, 1983.

N. Lossky, J. Míguez Bonino, J. Pobee, T. Stransky, G. Wainwright, P. Webb, eds, *Dictionary of the Ecumenical Movement*, Geneva, WCC Publications, 1991.

Luther, M., *Werke, Kritische Gesamtausgabe*, Weimar ed., 1833s.

Manschreck, Clyde L., transl. and ed., *Melanchthon on Christian Doctrine*, New York, Oxford UP, 1965.

Maurer, W., "Erasmus und das kanonische Recht", in *Vierhundertfünfzig Jahre lutherische Reformation*, Junghans, H. Ludalphi, eds, Berlin/Göttingen, Meier, 1967.

Mehl, R., *Catholic Ethics and Protestant Ethics*, Philadelphia, Westminster, 1971.

Mehl, R., "Law", in *Dictionary of the Ecumenical Movement*, pp.596-600 (see Lossky et al.).

Mehlhausen, J., "Schrift und Bekenntnis", in *Das Recht der Kirche*, vol. 1, pp.417-48 (see Rau et al.).

Melanchthon, Ph., "Apology of the Augsburg Confession, Art. II Original Sin", in Theodore G. Tappart, transl. and ed., *The Book of Concord*, Philadelphia, Muhlenberg, 1959.

Metz, R., "History of Canon Law", in *The New Catholic Encyclopedia*, vol. III, New York, McGraw-Hill, 1967, pp.34-50.

Meyer, Harding, Vischer, Lukas, eds, *Growth in Agreement: Reports and Agreed Statements of Ecumenical Conversations on a World Level*, Geneva, WCC, 1984.

Morris, C., "Christian Civilization", in *The Oxford Illustrated History of Christianity*, John McManners, ed., Oxford, Oxford UP, 1992, pp.196-233.

Nederveen Pieterse, J.P., *Empire and Emancipation: Power and Liberation on a World Scale*, London, Praeger, 1989.

Observations on the Pre-Gratian Canonical Collections: Actes du Congrès de Droit Canonique médiéval, J.J. Ryan, ed., Louvain, Ed. Universitaires, 1958.

O'Callaghan, Paul, *Fides Christi: The Justification Debate*, Dublin, Four Courts, 1997.

Ontwerp – Kerk Orde van de Verenigde Protestantse Kerk in Nederland, 1997.

Opocensky, Milan, ed., *Towards a Renewed Dialogue: Consultation on the First and Second Reformations*, Studies from the World Alliance of Reformed Churches, Geneva, WARC, 1996.

Örsy, L., *Theology and Canon Law: New Horizons for Legislation and Interpretation*, Collegeville MN, Liturgical Press, 1992.

Papadakis, A., "History of the Orthodox Church", in *A Companion to the Greek Orthodox Church*, Fotios K. Litsas, ed., New York, Greek Orthodox Archdiocese of North and South America, 1984, pp.7-31.

Paton, David M., ed., *Breaking Barriers: Nairobi, 1975. Official Report of the Fifth Assembly of the World Council of Churches*, London, SPCK, 1976.

Patsavos L., "The Canonical Tradition of the Orthodox Church", in *A Companion to the Greek Orthodox Church* (see Aghiorgoussis).

Phidas, Vlassios I., *Droit canon: Une perspective orthodoxe*, Analecta Chambesiana 1, Geneva, Centre orthodoxe du Patriarcat oecuménique, 1998.

Pirson, D., "Die Ökumenizität des Kirchenrechts", in *Das Recht der Kirche*, vol. I, 1997, pp.499-517 (see Rau et al.).

Pirson, D., "Die Rechtsnatur des Ökumenischen Rates der Kirchen", in *Universalität und Partikularität der Kirche*, München, Claudius, 1965, pp.302-24.

Pirson, D., *Universalität und Partikularität der Kirche*, München, Claudius, 1965.

Pottmeyer, Hermann J., *Towards a Papacy in Communion: Perspectives from Vatican Councils I and II*, New York, Crossroad, 1998.

"The Primacy of the Successor of Peter in the Mystery of the Church: Reflections of the Congregation for the Doctrine of the Faith", in *L'Osservatore Romano*, English ed., 18 Nov. 1998.

Raiser, K., "Report of the General Secretary", in *Together on the Way: Official Report of the Eighth Assembly of the World Council of Churches*, Harare, Dec. 1998, Diane Kessler, ed., Geneva, WCC, 1999, pp.81-102.

Raiser, K., "Which Steps in Ecumenism Are Overdue, Feasible and Desirable?", paper given at an ecumenical symposium in Trier, 11 April 1996, *The Ecumenical Review*, vol. 49, no. 2, April 1997.

Rasmussen, L.L., *Moral Fragments and Moral Community: A Proposal for Church in Society*, Minneapolis, Fortress, 1993.

Rau, Gerhard, Reuter, Hans-Richard, Schlaich, Klaus, eds, *Das Recht der Kirche*, 4 vols, Gütersloh, Chr. Kaiser, 1994-97.

"Relationships with Partners in the Ecumenical Movement, Churches Outside of the WCC Membership and Other Bodies", in *Towards a Common Understanding and Vision of the World Council of Churches*, pp.21-24.

"Report of the Sixth International Consultation of United and Uniting Churches (21-29 March 1995)", in *Built Together: The Present Vocation of United and Uniting Churches*, Thomas F. Best, ed., Faith and Order Paper no. 174, Geneva, WCC, 1997, pp.6-31.

Reuter, H-R., "Der Begriff der Kirche in theologischer Sicht", in *Das Recht der Kirche*, vol. 1, 1997, pp.23-75 (see Rau et al.).

Reuver, M., *Christians as Peacemakers: Peace Movements in Europe and the USA*, Geneva, WCC Publications, 1988.

Reuver, M., "The People of God and the Conciliar Process", in *Between the Flood and the Rainbow*, D. Preman Niles, ed., Geneva, WCC Publications, 1992, pp.26-33.

Reuver, M., *Requiem for Constantine*, Kampen, Kok, 1996.

Reuver, M. and Solms, Fr., *Churches as Peacemakers?*, Rome, IDOC International, 1985.

Ritter, A.M., *Einheit der Kirche in vorkonstantinischer Zeit*, F. von Lilienfeld, ed., Erlangen, K.C. Felmy & F. v. Lilienfeld, 1989.

Ritter, A.M., "Reich und Konzil", in *Das Recht der Kirche*, pp.36-58 (see Rau et al.).

Ruf, N., *Das Recht der Katholischen Kirche nach dem neuen Codex Iuris Canonici: für die Praxis erläutert*, Freiburg/Basel/Vienna, Herder, 1983.

Schieffer, Elisabeth, *Von Schauenburg nach Leuenberg. Entstehung und Bedeutung der Konkordie reformatorischer Kirchen in Europa*, Paderborn, Bonifatius, 1983.

Schillebeeckx, Edward, *Church: The Human Story of God*, London, SCM Press, 1990.

Sesboüé, B., "Le ministère de communion du pape", in *Etudes*, June 1996, pp.805-808.

Sprenger, Jakob, Heinrich Institoris, *Der Hexenhammer (= Malleus maleficarum)*, J.W.R. Schmidt, ed., Münich, Deutscher Taschenbuch, 1993.

Stein, A., "Herrschaft Christi und geschwisterliche Gemeinde", in *Das Recht der Kirche*, vol. 2, 1995, pp.272-317 (see Rau et al.).

Stierle, Wolfram, Werner, Dietrich, Heider, Martin, eds, *Ethik für das Leben: 100 Jahre ökumenische Wirtschafts- und Sozialethik*, Rothenburg, Ernst Lange Institut für ökumenische Studien, 1996.

Strohm, Chr., "Jus Divinum und Jus Lumanum, Reformatorische Begründung des Kirchenrechts", in *Das Recht der Kirche*, vol. 2, 1995, pp.115-73 (see Rau et al.).

Thurian, M., "Baptism, Eucharist and Ministry", in *Dictionary of the Ecumenical Movement*, pp.80-83 (see Lossky et al.).

Tillard, J.-M., *L'Eglise locale, ecclésiologie de communion et catholicité*, Paris, Cerf, 1995.

Tillard, J.-M., *Eglise d'Eglises: L'ecclésiologie de communion*, Paris, Cerf, 1987.

"Toronto Statement", in *Towards a Common Understanding and Vision of the World Council of Churches*, p.8.

Towards a Common Understanding and Vision of the World Council of Churches, Geneva, WCC, Geneva, 1997.

Tuchman, Barbara, *A Distant Mirror: The Calamitous 14th Century*, London, Papermac, 1995.

Vischer, L. "Kirchenrecht und Ökumenische Bewegung", in *Reformatio*, June 1975, pp.359-72.

Wainwright, Geoffrey, "Church", in *Dictionary of the Ecumenical Movement*, pp.159-67 (see Lossky et al.).

Ware, Kallistos Timothy, *The Orthodox Church*, Harmondsworth, UK, Penguin, 1993.

Weatherhead, James L., ed., *The Constitution and Laws of the Church of Scotland*, Edinburgh, Board of Practice and Procedure, 1997.